Also by Clyde Bolton

Nonfiction

The Crimson Tide (1972)
War Eagle (1973)
Unforgettable Days in Southern Football (1974)
Bolton's Best Stories of Auto Racing (1975)
The Basketball Tide (1977)
They Wore Crimson (1979)
Silver Britches (1982)
Remembering Davey (1993)
The Alabama Gang (1994)
Talladega Superspeedway (1994)
Stop the Presses (So I Can Get Off) (2005)

Novels

Water Oaks (1980)
Ivy (1986)
And Now I See (1989)
The Lost Sunshine (1994)
Nancy Swimmer, A Story of the Cherokee Nation (1999)
Turn Left on Green (2002)

HADACOL DAYS

A Southern Boyhood

A MEMOIR BY

CLYDE BOLTON

NEWSOUTH BOOKS

Montgomery | Louisville

NewSouth Books
105 S. Court Street
Montgomery, AL 36104

Published in the United States by NewSouth Books, a division of NewSouth, Inc., Montgomery, Alabama.

Library of Congress Cataloging-in-Publication Data

Bolton, Clyde.
Hadacol days : a southern boyhood : a memoir / by Clyde Bolton.
p. cm.
ISBN-13: 978-1-58838-200-9
ISBN-10: 1-58838-200-1
1. Bolton, Clyde—Childhood and youth. 2. Authors, American—20th century—Biography. I. Title.
PS3552.O5877Z46 2010
818'.5409—dc22
[B]

2010013310

Printed in the United States of America
by Sheridan Books

To the boys and girls of our little gang,
present and absent.

Chapter 1

There is a question I hate to hear because there is no simple answer: Where are you from?

Well, I was born in Anderson County Hospital in Anderson, South Carolina, on August 31,1936. At the time, my parents lived in nearby Williamston. I grew up in Williamston, Greenville, Edgemoor, Chester, Greenwood, and Clinton in South Carolina, Lawrenceville, Atlanta, Tucker, Statham, and Winder in Georgia, and Wellington in Alabama. As an adult I have lived in LaGrange in Georgia, and Gadsden, Montgomery, Birmingham, and Trussville in Alabama.

I attended ten schools, including three high schools. As they say in baseball, I had a cup of coffee at Jacksonville State University, so that makes eleven. One day I challenged my memory and recollected that I have lived in thirty-four dwellings, ranging from my present spacious nine-room home with three bathrooms to nondescript furnished apartments to a claustrophobic house trailer.

The three bathrooms are all indoors. It is necessary that I point that out because when I was a boy in Wellington our domicile was a four-room crackerbox with an outdoor toilet. I used to swap outdoor toilet stories wih Mike Lude, the Michigan native who became director of athletics at Auburn University. "You can't appreciate an indoor toilet until you've been to an outdoor toilet in Michigan in January," he told me. "You can't appreciate an indoor toilet until you've been to an outdoor toilet in Alabama in July," I told him.

So as a lad I was exposed to the bustle of Atlanta, to cafe philosophers in Statham, and to the lonesome hoot of the owl in Wellington, which isn't even a village but a vaguely defined rural area in Calhoun County. I am either a city boy, a small-town boy, or a country boy. Or all of the above. When asked the dreaded question of where I am from, it usually serves my purposes to answer either Statham or Calhoun County. I lived in Statham just three years, but I have written three novels in which it is the setting. Statham is called "Hempstead" in *Water Oaks*, *Ivy*, and *The Lost Sunshine*. I have been an Alabamian for five decades, so for the sake of clarity I frequently say I'm from Calhoun County.

The travel agents in my nomadic boyhood were my parents, Clyde Burnell Bolton Sr. and Annice Storey Bolton. Daddy was a railroad man, a depot agent for the Seaboard Air Line Railway. As a child I accepted the standard explanation that it was necessary that we move so that my daddy could better himself in his occupation. But after I acquired the judgment of an adult I realized there was more to it than that. It was obvious some of his career moves were simply sideways, not upward. I think my folks were restless, footloose types who enjoyed pitching their tent in a new town. The railroad would move their belongings for free, and there was a sense of adventure in unloading their sticks from a boxcar onto the platform of an unfamiliar depot in an unfamiliar town.

I had good parents who loved each other and who loved my sister, Betty, and me. They were role models in many ways. But all that confounded moving kept me constantly off balance, kept my emotions in a tangle. I was a dutiful child of the 1940s and 1950s, one who didn't complain. I should have complained, told them I didn't want to leave my friends, didn't want to have to make new friends. Maybe if I had been a squeaking wheel I would have gotten some grease. Years later, when I was a man and the cotton blond hair that gave me the nickname "Bunny" had given way to skin, I told my mother how I felt about being packed from town to town, school to school. She seemed genuinely shocked. "Betty," she said to my sister, "Bunny said he hated all the moving we did over the years. Did it bother you?" Betty gazed at her for a moment and then answered painfully, "Why, Mother, of course it bothered me."

Yet, I tell myself all the moving must have had some beneficial effect on my development. I learned to entertain myself, to play alone, to lose myself in my imagination as I shot at villains with my Buck Rogers zap gun or maneuvered toy soldiers across a rug. Maybe that prepared me to be a writer. I'm a fairly stoic fellow who isn't overwhelmed or even surprised when something goes wrong, and maybe the disappointment of constantly leaving my friends better prepared me to deal with disappointment as an adult.

But if you're asking me if I recommend moving kids from town to town, school to school, the answer isn't just no, but hell, no.

MY EARLIEST MEMORY is of falling on a hot furnace grate in the floor of our apartment in Greenville when I was a baby. I had on training pants but no shirt, and the result was an angry pink checkered pattern on my chest. To get my mind off the burns, my parents took me to the airport to watch planes take off and land.

In Lawrenceville we lived next door to my grandparents, Dorsey and Netta Bolton. I was a preschooler, and my grandmother and I plotted to deceive my mother. Mother insisted that she and I take a nap every afternoon, but as we lay on the bed I would hypnotize her, repeating the words I'd heard on a radio program. Once she was under my spell I would escape to my grandmother's house, and she would laugh conspiratorially when I'd tell her what I'd done. It was a daily occurrence. Mother, of course, was pleased to be rid of me for the afternoon so she could take a real nap.

"Let's kill Hitler," I'd regularly suggest to Mamma (that's what I called my grandmother), and I'd sit on her lap on the front porch, and we'd think up the most sadistic executions imaginable. I had seen a pig barbecued on a spit, and that was my favorite suggestion as to Adolf's fate.

In another early memory, my sister, Betty, who was ten years older than me, graciously agreed to take me on an outing with some of her teenaged Lawrenceville friends. We went to one of those lakes with a man-made beach that used to be so popular. While she swam I filled her rubber beach shoes with tadpoles. When she stepped into the shoes she didn't think it was a tad funny, and she was doubly irritated when her friends laughed. "I'll never take you anywhere else," she vowed. But she did.

Edgemoor was a delightful place for a preschool lad. Military maneuvers were conducted nearby, and soldiers and equipment arrived by train at Daddy's depot. The sight of so many uniformed men and tanks and guns and other martial apparatus was a constant reminder to adults that World War II raged on, but all I saw were heroes who gave me soldier caps and insignia and let me wear their helmets and ride in their Jeeps.

The residents of the village invited homesick soldiers from Wisconsin and Maine and Virginia and Minnesota into their homes for meals and fellowship. As the depot agent, my daddy took care of the army's needs, and soldiers frequently gave him whole hams and roasts. He'd bring the delicacies home with a story attached. "The fellow's name is Minelli," he'd say. "Italian boy. From Brooklyn, New York. Imagine that, the same Brooklyn where the Dodgers play. I asked him how he liked Edgemoor, and he said, 'Looks just like Brooklyn to me.' We both got a good laugh out of that."

Daddy wasn't so cordial when a couple of soldiers from New Jersey who had eaten with us several times suggested he let them borrow our family car to take my sister, Betty, a high school girl, to a movie in nearby Rock Hill. "Hell, no," he said, and they knew they'd overstayed their welcome. That story was told many times over the decades as our family reviewed snapshots from maneuver days in Edgemoor.

I acquired a scar when we lived in Edgemoor, and over the years I've made the most of it. I have but to mention it in a convivial setting and a chorus of "let's see it" arises. I am the only person I know who has a scar from a monkey bite. When I was a little boy we went to a farm to buy vegetables. A pet monkey was tethered to a pole. I had seen monkeys on organ grinders' shoulders in movies and books but when I tried to hoist this monkey to my shoulder he ripped my knee open with his fangs.

I started to school in Chester and on my first day claimed my first sweetheart. She was a twin. How did I tell her from her sister? It was simple: she was the one with the Band-Aid on her leg. Of course, she peeled off the Band-Aid in a couple of days, and I gave up on telling her from her sister and, indeed, on having a twin for a sweetheart.

It bugs me that I can't remember where I lived in Chester. I remember vividly all the other houses I lived in after I started to school and several before I entered school, but I'm blank on that one. No doubt it was rented, because we were serial renters. I have a report card from Chester. It shows that I attended Foote Street School just two of the school year's six terms. At the bottom is written this portentous message: "Clyde Bolton has moved to Greenwood, S.C."

In Greenwood we lived in an apartment in a huge old two-story wooden house of the kind that used to be commonplace in small towns when families were large. There must have been a dozen rooms in that thing. The green roof was broken up into geometric marvels, and adjacent to the porch there was even a covered area in which residents could get out of their cars—or buggies—on rainy days without getting wet. But its best days were past, and it had been divided into apartments.

We were living in that apartment when I picked out my little dog, Scooter, from among his siblings. He was half Boston bull and half Pekingese, black with a white streak down his chest, and my delightful companion for years. The first few nights he slept in Daddy's bedroom slipper, and we fed him with an eyedropper. I got him when I was in the first grade, and he died when I was in the twelfth grade. If Scooter hated moving he never showed it. He was happy wherever I was, and he adapted to new places after a couple of days of exploration. Like my parents, he regarded moving as an adventure.

I walked across the campus of Lander College to school in Greenwood. The female college students, pretty in shorts and white blouses, shot arrows at big straw-stuffed, multi-colored bull's-eyes on an archery range, and they'd occasionally offer me a turn with a bow. Alas, I didn't have the size or the strength to reach the targets.

We moved across town to a rented house. The good news was that it was on the same block as a handsome brick school. The bad news was that with the move I had to change schools. I was in my third school, and I was still in the first grade. I developed a close friendship with a boy who lived a few doors down the street, but we had to be quiet in his house because his father was frequently sprawled across a cot and snoring like a tornado. My parents stopped me from visiting, and when I pressed them for a reason they told me my pal's daddy was a drunk.

We moved to Atlanta, and we were back in an apartment. But not for long; we left the apartment for a rented house on Hemphill Avenue, and I changed schools. I was in the second grade, and I was attending my fifth school. That's a lot for the psyche of a child to handle. The school, Home Park, was a few blocks from the Georgia Tech campus. The Hemphill Avenue house has since been divided into apartments. At least it hasn't been torn down, as have so many of the schools and houses of my life.

THE DOGS OF World War II were snarling, and the students of Home Park were challenged to collect old newspapers and other paper for the war effort. We were divided into two teams, Army vs. Navy. I took it seriously and pestered my parents and neighbors for their newspapers, impatiently checking several times of an evening to see if Daddy was finished with the *Atlanta Journal*. My team won, but I don't remember whether I was Army or Navy.

The war provided us a background to play soldier, sailor, aviator, commando, spy. I still have mixed emotions when I see a Mitsubishi automobile on an American street because I remember shooting down dozens of Mitsubishi Zeroes from my backyard and saving Hemphill Avenue from the Japanese.

I had access to the greatest toy a kid ever enjoyed. The father of a boy who lived a few doors up the street from us owned a Piper Cub. The wings were removed so it would fit in the garage. The man let us play in the thing, a real airplane.

I had a crush on two girls in the third grade at Home Park, a smiley blonde named Mickey Allison and a dark-haired girl named Nancy West. (I don't think the crush was reciprocal in either case.) I was awed by Nancy because her picture had been in the *Atlanta Journal Magazine* for something or other. That made her a celebrity.

My sister, Betty, worked at Bell Aircraft in Marietta, and every payday I would be waiting for her at the foot of our steep driveway. She'd get off the city bus and hand me a dollar. It was a ritual. I took her largesse for granted, as kids will, but when I think back on it I realize she was a philanthropist because a buck then was a significant deduction from what must have been a small salary.

Betty, my only sibling, was eighteen years old when she married Harry Phares, a soldier from Ohio. I was eight, and I was awed when he moved into 1131 Hemphill Avenue with us. Harry dutifully took me to a downtown theater that showed cowboy B movies and ate the icky cereal that I talked Mother into buying just so I could have the premiums—plastic rings, badges, secret club memberships and such—that could be earned by mailing in box tops.

My dog, Scooter, was a cordial fellow—except when he was eating. You'd better leave him alone when he was chowing down. He was gnawing on a bone and baring his white teeth while I aggravated him one night. "Why,

Scooter wouldn't bite me," Harry said, and he reached for the bone. Scooter not only bit him, he did some tape-and-bandage damage.

Harry had served overseas, and he told my sister he would tell her all about it, that she could ask any question—but that he would never talk about it again. Turns out he had been part of a party that raided a German gasoline installation. Harry slipped up behind a guard and cut his throat. It was difficult for me to picture my calm, considerate brother-in-law slicing someone's gullet.

OF ALL THE places we lived, Mother was happiest in Atlanta. She and I would board the city bus in front of our house and get off downtown on Peachtree Street. Street photographers trolled that famous boulevard, and they'd snap pedestrians' pictures and mail the developed photos to their homes for a fee. I have such a picture of Mother and me. Don't tell anyone, but I'm wearing knickers.

Mother and I would go to Rich's and Davison's department stores and to dime stores and to my favorite, the Trick Novelty Shop, which sold such standards as pepper-flavored chewing gum, a buzzer that shocked the victim when you shook hands, a lapel flower that squirted water, and X-ray eyeglasses that promised much but delivered nothing. Mostly we didn't buy, we just looked.

We'd eat the special at Woolworth's, a turkey lunch, and she'd make the supreme sacrifice by taking me to the Capitol Theater. Loew's Grand could have its *Gone With the Wind*; the Capitol was home to Frankenstein, the Mummy, Dracula, the Wolf Man, all the scary guys.

Occasionally I'd ride the bus to downtown Atlanta by myself and hit the stores and go to a movie. You think this country hasn't changed? How long do you think an eight-year-old boy alone in downtown Atlanta would last today?

Mother was in South Carolina helping care for her ill mother on April

12, 1945, when President Franklin Delano Roosevelt died. I wrote her a letter catching her up on all my adventures and told her to hurry home and added: "I guess you heard about President Roosevelt." She kept that letter the rest of her life, and I still have it.

I liked Atlanta, but the inevitable day came when my parents announced we were moving, this time to Clinton. Years later I would be told the reason. Daddy had been a depot agent in our small towns, but he was a dispatcher in Atlanta, which was the railroad equivalent of an air traffic controller. He almost caused the wreck of a troop train. "It worried him to death," Mother told me. "He said he had to get away from the strain of dispatching."

Again, we lived in an apartment and in a rented house in Clinton. The house was on Florida Street, and the school was named Florida Street School, which seemed dumb to me. Why a Florida Street in South Carolina? At least I didn't have to swap schools when we moved out of the apartment and into the house. I was grateful for that. Still, I was in my sixth school and I was just a fourth grader.

I still get chills when I remember a neighbor, a kid my age, standing barefoot on a gallon jar that lay on its side. "You shouldn't do that," I said, "because that thing might break." I barely finished the sentence before it did break. His foot was a mess, and he was in the pits for a month during summer fun time.

Our next stop was Tucker—but there was a detour. Housing was scarce after the war, what with all the returning servicemen, and for a few months we stayed with Betty and Harry and their baby daughter, Cheryl, in a tiny basement apartment in Atlanta. "We've come to live with you," I announced cheerily. The young couple must have blanched at hearing those words.

Six decades later I still remember a strange experience I had in that apartment. My parents and Betty and Harry played cards most nights. I couldn't see anyone's hand but, oh, eight out of ten times I knew which suit would be trumps before it was called. I believe many of us have psychic abilities that go undeveloped or unrecognized. Their apartment was across the street from Grant Park, and I had a ball. I found Civil War bullets and visited the Cyclorama, the massive painting of the Battle of Atlanta, and I watched the attendants feed breakfast to the animals at the zoo. If there was an admission charge it never applied to me, and the zookeepers knew me by sight.

When school started in Tucker I rolled out of bed before daylight and rode with Daddy from Atlanta to the depot. I had a half hour to kill before I walked the two blocks to school, so I read *Black Beauty*. We finally got a house in Tucker. It was a dump, an old railroad section house that had to be fumigated before it was fit for occupancy. But kids are resilient, and because there was a huge tree to climb in the front yard and a red mud hill to slide down in a cardboard box, I liked the place. I was a passionate constructor of model war planes, the kind that required time and effort, with balsa wood frames and tissue paper coverings. I suspended them from my bedroom ceiling with sewing thread and lay on my back and gazed up at what I imagined to be heroes in pursuit of bad guys.

Fifth grade, seventh school, in case you're keeping score.

DADDY HAD A house built in Tucker, and for the first time we owned our home. Or at least the bank did. He and mother did much of the work themselves, such as hanging the sheetrock. Then he sold it for a profit and had another one built next door. High cotton for the Boltons, though it wouldn't last.

It was at Tucker, which is near Atlanta, that I discovered sports. Daddy took me to Ponce de Leon Park to see the Atlanta Crackers minor league baseball team play, and I attended the football and basketball games of the Tucker High Tigers. DeKalb County is practically a nation now, but in those days it was so sparsely populated that the high schools played six-man football.

I developed an exquisitely painful crush on an Older Woman. I can't even remember her name, but I worshiped her from across the chasm of six years' difference in age. She was a member of the Tucker High basketball team, and during a timeout the coach gave the players sections of quartered oranges. She ate hers and tossed the peel behind the bench. After the game I surreptitiously transferred the sacred relic to my jacket pocket. For the longest, I kept that orange peel in a drawer in my room.

There were no organized sports for little kids in Tucker in those days, so I erected a makeshift basketball goal (a bottomless ten-gallon lard can that flattened against the backboard when struck head-on by the ball) in my backyard. My pals Kelly Mansfield and Charles Stowers and I marked off a baseball field in a clearing in the woods and imagined the bushes in left field were the bleachers of Ponce de Leon Park, a distant home run target. We roped off a boxing ring in a shed behind Charles's house and used our ugly winter mittens for gloves.

I once wrote in a column in the *Birmingham News* that when I was a boy there were no Little League-type sports where I lived, and I added: "Thank God." I recalled the unorganized baseball, football, and basketball games of my childhood which were purely fun, with no adult meddling. But in recent years I have altered my views. In the declining United States in which we live today, organized sports for children are worthwhile—because the alternative isn't necessarily unorganized sports. Better the children are being regimented than being inundated by the constant flow of filth on television or being seduced by the scum of the earth—namely, drug dealers.

The object of my puppy love in Tucker was June Brown, a pigtailed classmate who regarded me merely as a friend. One day on the playground I summoned my courage and tried to kiss her. Our female teacher didn't think that was sweet, cute or funny. She thought it was just this side of a capital crime, and she threatened to haul me to the principal's office. Oh, well, I guess the teacher wasn't the romantic type.

It was in Tucker that I accepted Christ as my savior. I was eleven years old, but I knew what I was doing. I wasn't afraid when I was immersed in the baptistery at First Baptist Church. I felt wonderful, like you're supposed to feel.

My life could have ended when we lived in Tucker. I was a Cub Scout, and a group of us camped out at a lake. Someone had left a boat and trailer on a cement ramp that led into the water. I couldn't swim, but the water appeared shallow. Instead, there was a sharp drop-off at the end of the ramp. I jumped from the back of the boat and sank to the bottom in seven-foot water.

Everyone had left the area except me and one older boy—who, thank God, could swim. He saw me thrashing against the water and bounded into the lake to rescue me. I clamped my arms against his neck and pulled us both under. He was strong enough, though, to maneuver my dead weight (oops, poor choice of words) to shallow water. We Cub Scouts camped out under the stars that night, but I never went to sleep.

So I survived to move again. But this time it was to a place that holds my heart in a snare as tender and secure today as it was when it caught me in 1948.

That town is Statham, Georgia.

Chapter 2

It is 2010 and I am seventy-four years old. I haven't lived in Statham since 1951 when I was fifteen. Yet, a genial homesickness that could best be articulated in poetry frequently falls upon me like a gentle rain.

Statham calls, and usually my only answer is a sigh, but at least once a year I motor the 208 miles from my home in Trussville, Alabama, to experience the bittersweetness of trying to recapture that which can't be recaptured. After all, I travel in a car, not a time machine.

A few years ago I took a bat and three baseballs with me. I stood at what used to be home plate on what used to be the Statham High School baseball diamond and, one by one, tossed up the balls, swung the bat—and found that I could still hit them to the outfield. I left the balls on the playground for children to find.

It was raining and muddy, and I suspect the people in the house next door to the school thought I was crazy, but I have long since passed the age at which I worry about what people think of me. I adopted a bit of philosophy from of all people, Andy Warhol. The pop artist erased many of his concerns with two words: "So what?"

I am a right-handed batter, but I purposely hit those baseballs into right field, the opposite field. There was a reason. One of the more satisfying moments of my modest athletic life involved a hit to that right field in 1950. What happened was so unlikely, so farfetched, that it still has the qualities of a dream when I recall it.

In those days each village and town was represented by a team of adults.

Air conditioning and TV have, for the most part, killed off "town teams," but they once were commonplace and sources of great community pride. Statham's town team played on Saturdays and Sundays in the Independent League, a circuit that included Athens, which had access to University of Georgia players during the summer and fielded strong clubs.

I was the thirteen-year-old batboy for the Statham town team on a Sunday afternoon when Athens arrived for a game. But several of the Statham men were on vacation, and only eight showed up to play. Players had to be registered with the league, and the Statham manager told the Athens manager the only way Statham could field a team would be if he agreed to let the batboy play under the name of one of the absent men. The Athens manager, knowing an easy out when he saw one, agreed, and I was penciled in to bat ninth, the traditional spot for the weakest hitter. On the mound was a University of Georgia pitcher. To make matters even more terrifying, his nickname was Ace.

I hauled my quaking carcass to the plate for my first at-bat against the redoubtable Ace. I wasn't uniformed like the rest of the players; I wore jeans, white T-shirt, and tennis shoes. I prayed that I wouldn't freeze, that I wouldn't turn into a pillar of salt, like Lot's wife, that I could at least get the bat off my shoulder and swing three times and sit down.

Strike one swinging. Strike two swinging. I swung the third time and, to my amazement, heard the bat hit the ball. I had swung late and sliced the ball over the first baseman's head. It landed fair by a foot and then spun across the foul line away from the right fielder. By the time he ran the ball down and returned it to the infield, I was perched on second base. I hadn't merely gotten a hit off Ace, I had doubled off Ace.

I struck out in every other appearance at the plate that day, but for one shining moment a thirteen-year-old eighth grader had conquered a Southeastern Conference pitcher.

Statham (it's pronounced State-um) is located on two-lane Business U.S. 29, fourteen miles west of Athens. It was simply Highway 29 during the three years we lived there, but it has been demoted, a bypass taking not only its traffic but its name. We moved there in 1948 and left in 1951. I was in the seventh, eighth, and ninth grades at Statham School. The 1950 census listed the population of the town as 626.

I was at home in Statham, and I realized it within days after we moved into a rented house near the depot where Daddy would be the station agent for the Seaboard railroad. The kids of the town accepted me with a healthy curiosity. Most had lived in Statham all their lives, and my travelogue of nine towns and seven schools intrigued them. They welcomed me into their adventures, into their homes, and onto their teams. There was a confluence of age, era, friends, and circumstances that gold-plated those years.

There were nine of us who lived within an easy bicycle ride of each other, who saw each other nearly every day. We were buddies and sweethearts and teammates and sharers of dreams. "Our little gang," I refer to them today, but we had no collective name back then. "Let's get everybody together for a weenie roast tonight," someone would say, and it was understood who "everybody" meant.

Our little gang consisted of Wayne Holliday, Jimmy Lowe, Chick Bragg, Buck Manus, Rose Marie Herrin, Gayle Mobley, Harriette Robertson, Emma Lou Owens and me. Jimmy and Chick were a year behind the rest of us in school.

Wayne's house was centrally located, at the corner of Broad and Jefferson streets, and it was our routine gathering place. His mother, Carrie, put up with us, sometimes with a sigh and a frown; as I realize now, she went beyond the call of duty. I'm sure she tired of the ongoing conflict that had Wayne's little sister, Janet, wanting to be included in our adventures and our little gang leaving her behind.

Wayne's long, treeless backyard provided a perfect football field. "I'm

Charley Trippi," a quick thinker would "catch" before the game. The consolation prize: "I'm Frank Sinkwich." Once those two University of Georgia immortals were caught, there was no point in being anyone else. Sinkwich won the Heisman Trophy, but there were three reasons Trippi outranked him in our minds: (1) Trippi's last season at Georgia was 1946, just a couple of years before, while Sinkwich's was 1942. (2) Trippi was starring in pro football, and our little gang kept up with his exploits. Charley, who was headed to both the college and professional football halls of fame, had, in fact, led the Chicago Cardinals to the 1947 National Football League championship. (3) Trippi had also played baseball with our beloved Atlanta Crackers. (Three decades later, when I interviewed Trippi and Sinkwich for my book on Georgia football, *Silver Britches*, each got a good laugh out of our little gang's efforts to claim the privilege of being them.)

We played tackle football, never two-hand touch, but the only time I can remember anyone suffering a scary injury was in a game in Jimmy Lowe's front yard when I knocked Buck Manus into a concrete banister and he landed on his collarbone. We were afraid it was broken, but it wasn't. He did have a nasty bruise for several days.

Sometimes the girls would insist on playing football with us. Girls were girls and boys were boys back then, even on the football field, and we weren't going to level a female with a hard tackle or block. We caught them by the waist and playfully wrestled them to the ground (careful that our hands were properly placed). That approach worked with most, but it put us at a disadvantage with Gayle Mobley, who was as fast and shifty and determined as the boys.

Gayle and I were chatting one day in 2007, and she especially remembered one of those games. "We were playing football one day, and we had beaten Buck Manus and his team," she said. "I got on my bike and was going home, and that devil shot me in the back with a BB gun. He popped me a good one right in the back. I said, 'I'll go home and tell my mother, and she'll come and get you.' We fussed about that for the longest."

Wayne's backyard was too narrow for baseball. We'd usually pedal to the skinned, dusty diamond behind the high school for that. But one day we were batting at Wayne's when an older boy asked to play. He swung the bat, and, as if laser-directed, the ball found the window of a nearby house. The culprit vamoosed, leaving Wayne to face the music. Wayne's buddies loyally stayed with him, though.

WE PLAYED PICKUP basketball at the school gym, but basketball also provided our first taste of organized sport. Wayne and I were teammates on a succession of squads that, like rungs on a ladder, led to the high school varsity. Basketball was a big deal to the students and townspeople of Statham before the high school was closed in 1956.

The gym was a typical red brick building with wooden backboards (they're still wooden today), dressing rooms without showers, a scoreboard that required hand flipping of metal numbers, and room for some seven hundred spectators. At night the light spilled out from rows of side windows like pats of butter on black bread as the townspeople queued up to pack the stands for games against such arch rivals as Bogart, Winder, and Braselton. The gym was constructed by community effort—I mean hard, sweaty labor—when money was scarce in the early 1940s, and the people of Statham felt a proprietary interest in the building and its teams. Boys of athletic bent felt it was a near-sacred aspiration to someday play for the Statham High School Wildcats varsity. Wayne and I were such boys, and our friendship was forged as much by our togetherness on that court as anywhere else.

As adults, Wayne and I reminisced about those days and laughed about a unique yell of the Statham cheerleaders and how it inspired us. As we remembered it, we shifted into a higher gear when Joan Smith, Rose Marie Herrin, Joyce Marlowe, and Peggy Dunahoo yelled, "Statham Wildcats on the ball, they've been drinking Hadacol." It was the favorite refrain of the players and the fans.

My gosh, I still mutter it absentmindedly. My nine-year-old granddaughter, Hannah Bolton, has heard it so often that when I sing-song, "Statham Wildcats on the ball . . ." she chimes in with, "They've been drinking Hadacol."

What in the world was Hadacol? It was an elixir marketed as a vitamin supplement by a Louisiana politician named Dudley J. LeBlanc, and it found its way into Southern folklore. Its main attraction for many customers was that it contained twelve percent alcohol—the same as some wines. That didn't go unappreciated in the many dry counties of the South. Some pharmacies in dry counties even went so far as to sell Hadacol by the shot glass. In Chicago sales of the patent medicine were limited to liquor stores. It's easy to picture a teetotaling little old Statham lady who wouldn't think of drinking beer, wine, or whiskey having her dose of Hadacol before retiring.

Alas, Statham's trademark yell was doomed. Paul T. Barrett, the principal and coach, was not amused by the suggestion, even in fun, that his players were fueled by alcohol. "Mr. Barrett put a stop to it because he didn't like it," Joan Smith Hammond recalled. But she nevertheless gave me her rendition of the long version: "Statham Wildcats on the ball, they've been drinking Hadacol. Sound off, one, two. Sound off, one, two. Sound off, one, two, three, four. Sound off!" She added, "Isn't that silly?" and I told her I didn't think it was silly at all. I even thought that if Mr. Barrett was listening to our conversation from on high he might relent and laugh at her yell.

The very idea of Hadacol caught the fancy of the South. "Hadacol Boogie" became a popular recording. I still remember the tune. There was a Captain Hadacol comic book. LeBlanc's Hadacol Caravan was the last of the big-deal medicine shows. He enlisted Hank Williams, Jimmy Cagney, Jack Dempsey, Judy Garland, Minnie Pearl, Mickey Rooney, Lucille Ball, Milton Berle, George Burns and Gracie Allen, and Bob Hope to help him market Hadacol.

Finally, the Federal Trade Commission said that, in Hadacol, old Dudley had a dud. It spoke of "leeringly prurient ballyhoo" and said the publicity behind the tonic was "false, misleading and deceptive in representing the nostrum as an effective treatment and cure for scores of ailments and diseases."

The other day I read that Hadacol bottles and related items are prized among collectors of Southern memorabilia and medical quackery today. Good, because a few months before, in an antique mall, I had found a bottle of Hadacol and bought it. It's two-thirds full. All the vitamins and minerals are listed on the label, which also declares the twelve percent alcohol as a "preservative."

The last time I was in Statham my heart sank when I noticed that Wayne's house had gone the way of Hadacol. The Baptist church next door—the church Wayne had loved and served as boy and man—had bought the property and torn down the house. I long ago came to terms with the thirty-five-foot trees that transformed Wayne's backyard from a football field into a pine grove, but destroying the house, the de facto headquarters of our little gang? I felt as if a historic edifice had been torn down, as if Mount Vernon or Monticello had given way to the bulldozer.

I think Wayne was the best of us. He never cussed, which set him apart from most boys who thought profanity made them seem tough and grown up. He never even joined in our adolescent, lurid remarks about females. As an adult he would serve the Statham Baptist Church as deacon, Sunday school teacher, Training Union director, and choir member.

There was one bizarre occasion when he would have been justified in stringing together a dictionary of expletives, but he didn't. The Statham High School baseball team was practicing. Wayne, a left-handed hitter, was at bat and a runner was on first base. Smokey Stover, the catcher, attempted a pickoff play. Only trouble, the throw went no more than a couple of feet.

The ball hit Wayne point-blank in the back of the head—and this was before batting helmets.

We were all too stunned to move at first. Had we really seen what we had just seen? Then the players and Mr. Barrett, the coach, ran to Wayne's side. "Are you all right? Are you all right? Are you all right?" (Why do people always ask if an injured person is all right when it's obvious he isn't?)

Wayne's lip was quivering, and he was trying not to cry in front of the team. He shoved us away, turned his back on us, and walked past the pitcher's mound, to the basepath between first and second. We followed, asking him if he was all right, as he pushed us away and headed toward third base. More of the same, his teammates pleading with him and Wayne heading now for home plate, where stunned Smokey Stover stood with his mitt on one hand and his catcher's mask in the other. Wayne stopped, looked him in the eye, and all he said was, "Shoot fire, Smokey!"

Wayne thus made baseball history in Statham. He also made theatrical history. He had but one word in a class play. He was supposed to run onto the stage and shout, "Hoorah!" His big moment came, and he bounded from the wings and yelled, "Rah-hoo!"

Wayne had a middle-sized yellow dog named Jack that had an extra toe on each foot. He had a pet crow named Bill. (There was an older boy in town named Bill Crowe, and that's how Bill the crow got his name. Pretty clever on Wayne's part.)

One day the members of our little gang pitched in to buy the essentials for a weenie roast. Harriette Robertson went to the grocery store and returned to Wayne's house with the weenies in the basket of her blue bicycle. They were in a paper sack, sold individually, not prepackaged as they are now. She laid the bike down and went inside to tell us she was back. As we started outside she screamed, "Jack's got the weenies!" We snatched a few of the weenies away from Jack, but we all looked at each other with curled lips and raised eyebrows that meant, "I ain't eating those things," so we tossed them back to the grateful canine thief, anted up again from our meager resources, and sent Harriette back to the store.

Wayne didn't keep Bill the crow in a cage. He was free to fly wherever he wanted to, but he always returned home. He'd sit attentively on Wayne's shoulder while we talked about Atlanta Crackers baseball, and we almost expected Bill to chime in with an opinion as to who should be playing shortstop.

Bill the crow was a cute curiosity, but he wasn't a favorite with the neighbors. Remember when milk was un-homogenized and delivered to homes in glass bottles with paper stoppers and the cream rose to the top? More than once I (and probably every other kid of pre-homogenization days) was scolded for drinking the rich cream and leaving the bland milk. Bill liked the cream, too, and he visited the neighbors' front porches after the milkman had made his run, pecked a hole in the top, and sucked out the cream. Townspeople had to weigh the inconvenience of having the milkman wake them early with a knock on the door against the possible theft of their cream by the larcenous Bill.

Wayne was my best friend, and I was his best friend. Once when I was throwing my pocketknife at a target on the ground it stuck in Wayne's foot. The blood flowed. I was crestfallen, apologetic. "It's all right," Wayne said. "Don't worry about it. I know you didn't mean to do it." That's the kind of friendship we had. But no friendship is perfect, and I still regret a moment of pettiness on my part.

Wooden steps led down a hill to an idyllic spring. It was a favorite picnicking spot for the townspeople. For the steps to fit the contour of the hill, there was a platform in the middle of the flight. I saw the platform as a ramp for a daredevil feat. I was going to be Evel Knievel before Evel Knievel was. I told Wayne I'd ride my bike down the steps and fire off the platform into the air and land on the hillside if he'd do the same. He agreed.

I performed the idiotic stunt, and the hard landing bent the fork of my bicycle. I was lucky it didn't bend me.

"I ain't doing that," Wayne said.

Misery loves company. "You've got to," I whined. "You said you would if I did." What I should have said was, "Don't do it, Wayne. There's no point in messing up your bike, too."

Wayne didn't jump. I called him chicken. I pushed my damaged bike the mile to my house, miffed at Wayne and feeling sorry for myself. It was not one of my more noble moments, and I don't excuse it by saying I was just a kid.

IN 2006 THERE was a reunion for those who attended Statham High School in the 1950s. I was pleased when Carolyn Holliday, Wayne's widow, introduced me as "Wayne's brother."

I moved to Alabama in 1952. As an adult Wayne joined the Air Force and left Statham. We grew apart, as happens so often with childhood friends. But he returned to the area, and our friendship bloomed again. When we were together we reminisced about our perfect time and perfect place.

In December 1976 Wayne learned he had cancer. His color was poor and he lost weight, but he underwent a colostomy, and when I saw him again he was happy and he appeared strong and healthy.

Life doesn't just knock you down, it piles on. Of all times for the hammer to fall: Wayne was happily shooting hoops with his daughter when his legs refused the command of his brain. The cancer had reoccurred.

He weighed less than a hundred pounds the last time I saw him. He needed to be moved from one room in his house to another, and big, strong Jimmy Lowe, one of our little gang, scooped him up and carried him in his outstretched arms as if he were a baby.

Before Wayne died I told him I loved him, and he told me he loved me. Clark Wayne Holliday was forty-one years old when he died on August 15, 1978. In his case, at least, it was true that the good die young.

Chapter 3

There is a scene in my novel, *Water Oaks*, in which four sweaty young male skinny-dippers arrive at a pond in the woods on a summer's day and spot a cottonmouth moccasin sunning itself on the dam. One of the boys chunks a rock at the snake, and it slithers off its weedy cushion and disappears into the pond. Then the four get naked and plunge into the restorative waters, paying no further mind to the cottonmouth.

An editor with a New York publisher who rejected my manuscript noted that the scene was ridiculous, that no one would be fool enough to shoo a poisonous snake into a pond and then get in there with the thing.

A few days later I was in Atlanta to cover the Peach Bowl football game for my newspaper, the *Birmingham News*, and I submitted the manuscript to the publishing house Cromartie-Long. The next morning, Bill Cromartie, one of the firm's founders, came to my motel and said the most welcome words an author will ever hear: "I stayed up until three o'clock this morning reading your manuscript. I couldn't put it down. We want to publish it."

What was the difference? I suspect the woman who found the snake story so preposterous lived in Manhattan or New Canaan, Connecticut, where the only moccasins are worn on the feet. Cromartie, on the other hand, grew up in Leesburg, a small town in southwest Georgia. Cottonmouths and ponds and naked boys swimming weren't unfamiliar to him.

Now, the facts are that when I was a lad my buddies and I were regular denizens of Perry's Pond in Statham, and we did throw rocks at cottonmouths on the dam—frequently there were three or four of the creatures—and they'd slide into the water, and then we'd fling our clothes aside and belly-bust the surface ourselves. You see, we thought snakes couldn't bite under water. We didn't reason that moccasins eat fish, and fish live in water. Maybe we were just lucky that we were never bitten by a cottonmouth.

My confidence that snakes wouldn't bite under water was one of several misapprehensions about nature that I entertained. I believed that a hoop snake had a poisonous horn on its head and that it became a hoop by biting its tail, and then it rolled in pursuit of its prey, horn at the ready. One fellow knew for a fact that a hoop snake rolled down a hill and accidentally stuck its horn in a tree, and the tree died in three days. I believed that porcupines shot their quills, that a snapping turtle that bit you wouldn't turn loose until sundown, and that if a frog peed on you a wart would grow to mark the spot. For good measure, let me add that I believed anyone eating fish and drinking milk would die, and the same fate would befall a person who consumed watermelon and whisky—although I can't conceive of anyone's taste running toward the latter combination.

We never fished in Perry's Pond. Perry's was for swimming (despite the No Swimming sign posted by the owners), and the larger Rozzie's Pond, with its overhanging bushes and inviting inlets, was for fishing. We didn't swim in Rozzie's because it was visible from Providence Road, and swimsuits would have been mandatory—and who wanted to be bothered by a swimsuit? The ponds were barely three hundred yards apart, but we assigned a separate use to each one.

There was a small wooden boat, complete with paddle, at Rozzie's. It was simply tied to a bush, never locked down. It was for the use of anyone who wanted to fish. The fishing was free and so was the boat. I don't even know who owned it. Fast forward to today and picture that scene. What would happen? Why, the boat either would be stolen and sold by drug addicts or destroyed by vandals. It wouldn't last a week.

My daddy had a couple of fishing rods that were at my disposal, but they had the old-style reels that spun the line into a bewildering tangle if you didn't apply your thumb at precisely the right moment. He was skillful, casting a plug under an overhanging bush, missing the low limbs by an inch, then expertly giving the rod just the right twitch to portray the lure as a wounded minnow. His tackle box was well outfitted, and he religiously filed his hooks to a needle point.

I hated those reels. I spent half my time unraveling the bird's nest that resulted in the mechanism when I tried to cast. I knew where there was a stand of bamboo, so I chose to fish with a cane pole and a cork (sometimes an actual cork from a medicine or wine bottle). There were legions of worms beneath the surface of our yard, and a few minutes of digging produced a day's supply of ammunition with which to attack the resident bream of Rozzie's Pond.

That's still the kind of fishing I prefer, the kind I taught myself at Rozzie's Pond. Oh, I did return to rods and reels, what with the popularity of the spinning reel, but I prefer a worm or a cricket and a quiet, isolated setting. Give me a baloney sandwich and a beer and a good book and I hope the fish won't disturb me by biting.

My son, Mike Bolton, is the outdoor editor of the *Birmingham News*, and he is the antithesis of the lazy fisherman. He has a bass boat with all the appurtenances, and the thing resembles a battleship. He is an expert on lake and sea. And, yes, he uses the type reel his granddaddy did, and it doesn't tangle with him, either. Mike seems happiest when the fishing is an ordeal. He and the late racecar drivers, Neil Bonnett and Dale Earnhardt Sr., were fishing and hunting buddies. One day Mike called me and said, "Neil and Dale and I are going fishing tomorrow, you want to come along?" I told him I would, but then he added, "We'll pick you up at 4:30 in the morning." I replied, "Not as long as Winn-Dixie has a fish counter, you won't."

The boys' state of undress precluded the girls of our little gang visiting Perry's

Pond, but they would occasionally grace Rozzie's Pond with their presence. They'd pull off their sandals and wade at the edge of the water, and when they'd lose a rock-skipping contest they'd say it wasn't fair because boys just naturally had stronger arms and could make rocks skip more times.

"Let's take a boat ride," I suggested to Rose Marie Herrin, and we did. I paddled until my shoulders ached, and we started back. But I stopped twenty yards short of the bank. "I'm not going to take you on in," I said. "We'll just stay here the rest of the day." Rose Marie—everybody called her Ree—was a cute, antic, round-faced cheerleader with pinpoint freckles and a voice like a chainsaw that needed oiling when directed at boys who were aggravating her. I knew my declaration would provoke the scolding yelp she reserved for such pimpled adversaries, and it did: "Clyde Bolton, you get me out of this boat right now!"

"Nope."

"I mean it. You paddle this thing to the bank or I'll start screaming."

"Scream."

She didn't have to scream. She spotted an old bait can in the bottom of the boat and began scooping water from the pond and throwing it on me. Nothing like stinking, rotten, liquefied worms to make a fellow paddle a boat. Why would I remember such an insignificant scene nearly six decades later? I don't know. The human mind is a strange contraption. It can forget the monumental and recall the inconsequential, the most trivial act or conversation.

I'm convinced that one of the great gifts God gives us is a negative—the inability to see into the future. If I had known on that day in that little rowboat on Rozzie's Pond that sweet Rose Marie would die in a fire when she was thirty-six years old . . . Well, thank God I didn't.

I've never experienced anything else quite as refreshing as a skinny-dip in Perry's Pond. Usually it followed a pickup baseball game on the skinned diamond behind the high school. We were sweating like hogs and covered with dust, and we slipped our smelly ball gloves over the handlebars and raced our bicycles down Providence Road for a half-mile and then over a rutted dirt road to the stream-fed pond, which probably was but a half-acre or so in size.

We tossed our jeans and T-shirts and ball caps and tennis shoes onto the brown straw that covered the ground in a well-kept pine grove and charged into the pond. The water was cold, and we knew it would hurt less if we hit it all at once rather than wade in inch by inch. When you opened your eyes under the water and raised them toward the surface you saw a sunny, light green opaqueness, and the world seemed made of jade.

We splashed each other and we ducked each other and we raced each other freestyle, backstroke, sidestroke, or any other stroke we could think of, and we pulled ancient sticks and bushes out of the gooey bottom with our toes and tossed them over the dam. Come to think of it, I don't believe the water in Perry's Pond was over our heads.

We didn't have towels, didn't want them, and when an hour or so of cavorting had passed we wrestled on twisted shirts and stuck our feet in squishy shoes and bicycled back up Providence Road, standing on the pedals because it was a tough uphill climb.

Not only did we swim in Perry's Pond on boiling Georgia summer days, the hardiest among us took a ceremonial dip each New Year's Day to prove how tough we were. Mother said it proved how insane we were.

I wrote three novels—*Water Oaks*, *Ivy*, and *The Lost Sunshine*—that were set in a small Georgia town in the 1950s. Its fictional name was Hempstead, and it was patterned on Statham. Prentice's Pond, my fictional Perry's Pond, is prominent in *Water Oaks* and *The Lost Sunshine.* After a Hollywood production company took an option on *Water Oaks*, the scriptwriter was so impressed with the importance of the pond in the story that she titled the potential movie *Prentice's Pond.* Alas, it remained "potential," for no film was ever made.

We were serial skinny-dippers. The climber who assaulted the mountain "because it was there" had nothing on us. The most unlikely, least accommodating puddle of water beckoned us.

There was a wet-weather stream near the town dump of such long duration that it had carved a mini-gorge, perhaps ten feet deep. During one of our explorations of the woods we spotted a pool in the gorge that was no larger than a bathroom and just waist deep, and after a heavy storm we'd head for that body of water and its fresh rainwater.

Once we came upon an open area that for some reason or other was being dynamited. The blasts dug craters that filled with Georgia-red muddy water and in which the pungent stink of recently spent dynamite lingered. Who would go swimming in a glorified mudhole that smelled bad? We would.

One day Buck Manus professed to have found a picturesque swimming hole in a creek that coursed through woods a couple of miles from town. We rode our bikes out Highway 29 and walked through the forest—and found that Buck's discovery was a smidgen of stream ten feet wide and two feet deep, with clean, clear water rippling over mossy rocks at either end. It was lovely to look at but suitable as a swimming hole only for little fish. But Buck was our pal, and we didn't upbraid him for his lapse in judgment. (Besides, Buck could take a pencil and without pressing write perfectly legible sentences on his arms, as if he were writing on a sheet of Blue Horse Notebook paper. None of the rest of us could do that, and we had great respect for the possessor of such an awesome talent.) We dropped prone in the creek and splashed water on each other, but we never returned. We'd take Perry's Pond, thank you, Buck.

MY WIFE, SANDRA, was impressed by Perry's Pond, too, though she never saw it. "You make skinny-dipping sound like so much fun, talking about it and writing about it in your novels," she said one night as we sat on the deck of our houseboat on Logan Martin Lake in Alabama. "I wish there was some way I could go skinny-dipping sometime, but I couldn't ever."

"What's wrong with right now?" I asked. "We could skinny-dip in a big old lake as well as we could in a little old pond."

"Are you crazy?" she said. "We'd get put in jail. No, absolutely no."

"It's late at night, there's no one around. No one could possibly see us. Come on, let's hit it."

"No, no, no. Still, it would be fun."

We turned off all the lights in and on the houseboat, shucked our clothes, and plunged naked into the bracing waters of Logan Martin Lake. Just a couple of fifty-six-year-old kids skinny-dipping.

"It's fun!" Sandra exclaimed, sputtering as she pushed herself to the surface. "It's just like you said."

In the late 1990s I made several trips to the site of New Echota, the old capital of the Cherokee Nation near Calhoun, Georgia, to do research for *Nancy Swimmer*, my novel about the shameful treatment of the Cherokees before, during, and after the Trail of Tears.

One day I was walking through the woods beside a creek when I came upon a rock-bound swimming hole that my guide brochure said was frequented by little Cherokee boys two centuries before. On the split screen of my mind I pictured Indian boys playing in a cold creek and white boys frolicking in a cold pond, both in Georgia, but separated by so much time and circumstance.

I decided to strip and hit that Cherokee swimming hole. If I did I could acquire first-hand atmosphere for my novel, and what a story to tell my friends and family. Those who aren't fully convinced I am crazy would be if I went skinny-dipping in a creek in a state park in Georgia.

But I lost my guts. I "looked at the big picture," as adults often do when they lose their guts. It was broad daylight. Suppose some female tourists strolled by—and saw the naked man and screamed and reported me to the uniformed park rangers? I could picture me before the judge. "I'm an author from Alabama, and I'm going to write a book about the Cherokees, and I was doing research."

"You do your research naked in a creek where passersby can see you?" the judge would ask.

"Well, er, in this case, yes, Your Honor."

What would the charge have been? Indecent exposure? Well, at least insanity might have worked as a defense. My book never would have been written. I would have been fired from my newspaper. I would have disgraced my family. I would be forever remembered as a pervert. Maybe it's a good thing I looked at the big picture—but I still think of it as an opportunity lost.

I was an adult working for the *Birmingham News* when I began to notice kudzu and other growths kidnapping the dirt road that led from Providence Road to Perry's Pond. Each year when I would return to Statham the overgrowth had become denser, and I knew our old mother church of skinny-dipping must be history. "Perry's Pond ain't there anymore," a townsman told me. "I'm not sure what happened to it."

Years later I vowed to myself that I would find the pond site. I was on my way to Athens to cover a football game, and I had on dress pants, but I plunged into what had become a jungle. I twisted and turned and pushed and wiped blood from brier scratches from my arms and swatted mosquitoes that attacked in squadrons. My polyester pants were picked and pulled and ruined. I sidestepped the poison ivy as best I could.

I came upon what had been the handsome, well-kept pine thicket on the slope just above the pond, where adults pitched their tablecloths and quilts for picnics. The sunless clump, its trees wired together by rogue vines, looked more like Poe's haunted woodland of Weir. I heard a chorus of bullfrogs, and I knew I was near whatever remained of Perry's Pond. I needed a machete, but I didn't have one, so I pushed on with a stick in my hand.

And there it was. A relic from a time long gone. The dam had burst, and the lowest part of the pond was a stinking swamp. Three turtles dived like submarines when they saw me. They weren't used to humans, and no wonder in that forlorn place. Thirty-foot pines and conversely stunted trees and bushes deprived of sunlight lived on the muddy floor of what used to be Perry's Pond.

I stood there a few minutes and remembered good clean days when the site was open and the pond reflected white clouds that floated in powder blue skies. Then I did the only thing I could do. I turned and fought my way back to Providence Road and drove to Athens to cover my ball game.

THE POPULATION OF Statham in 1950 was 626. The census recorded 2,040 folks in 2000 and estimated there'd be 2,555 in 2005. So you see what is happening to my little town. Subdivisions are sprouting everywhere. I assume its people work in Athens and are willing to drive twenty-eight miles round trip each day to live in a village. The pasture behind my old house on Broad Street is no longer a pasture; it's a neighborhood, and the residents can see into my backyard from their backyards. Come to think of it, you don't see many pastures anywhere anymore, do you?

Subdivisions are closing in on the acreage around our little gang's beloved body of water like Sherman closing in on Atlanta, and I suspect that one day the bulldozers and backhoes will arrive with clang and clatter, and the site of Perry's Pond will become a family's zoysia grass front lawn, and they will never know naked boys used to swim there.

Chapter 4

"Let's go see the Crackers play!" There was electricity in Daddy's voice when he spoke those words, and I was the perfect conductor. "Boy hidy, let's do!" I'd yelp, usually before he finished the sentence.

He enjoyed surprising me, and the invitation had the same effect as if he had produced a shiny gift from behind his back.

We'd board the family's 1940 Oldsmobile that too obviously had been repainted, Mother, Daddy and me, and head west on Highway 29. The car wasn't air conditioned, but I didn't care, for the only places I'd experienced air conditioning were movie theaters that advertised their magic climate with banners that hung from the marquees and featured the word "cool" capped with snow. In those days the side windows of cars were equipped with little wings that opened out and directed outside air inside. With all the windows open and air swirling and Mother's hair protected by a scarf, I put my chin on the back of the front seat and talked baseball with Daddy while smoke drifted from his ever-present unfiltered Camel cigarette. It was the only way I could tame my impatience for the two hours and fifty-five miles that separated Statham from my field of dreams. It was a tedious two-lane tour of small-town America through Russell, Winder, Carl, Auburn, Dacula, Lawrenceville, Tucker, Rehobeth, and Decatur, punctuated by traffic lights that were always red on our side and cars and pickups and transport trucks that conspired in delaying our arrival at the game for as long as possible. But the prize at the end of the journey was worth it.

Our destination was Ponce de Leon Park, home of the Atlanta Crackers (or Poncey, as the Atlanta sportswriters called it.) We'd spot the stadium lights against the night sky blocks away, and I'd say something like, "Isn't that grand?" and Daddy would agree that it surely was, and Mother would smile at the enthusiasm of her two men. We'd park in the lot of the massive Sears store across the street, Daddy would buy tickets, we'd twirl the turnstiles, they'd give me hot dog money and show me where they'd be sitting—and I'd tell them I'd meet them there in the ninth inning. I wanted to fully savor the experience by sitting behind home plate, beside first base, beside third base, along the outfield lines. Sometimes, when no usher was looking, I would slip into the expensive box seats.

It's difficult to explain to today's audience what the Atlanta Crackers meant to the people of Statham and other Georgia towns, large and small. Jimmy Carter understood, for he wrote about traveling from Plains to Poncey as a boy and thus becoming "the envy of our town."

The Class AA Southern Association experienced a fantastic boom after World War II, as did most of minor league baseball. The pinnacle was reached in 1949 when 464 teams in fifty-nine minor leagues pulled forty-two million fans. It was as if a massive "let's finally have some fun" switch were thrown in the minor league nation when the war ended. In 1946 the eight clubs of the Southern Association attracted 1,831,236 fans, easily breaking the old record of 1,351,570 set in 1925. The Crackers drew 395,695, highest in SA history.

What to do for an encore in 1947? Well, the league played to 2,180,344 and the Crackers, despite finishing fifth, to 404,584. The next year 21,812 came to 15,000-seat Poncey for the opener against Birmingham.

But numbers alone didn't do it justice. Fans in Statham and Athens and Watkinsville and Austell and Douglasville and Bethlehem (no, not that Bethlehem) sat by their radios and lived and died with the adventures of the Crackers. They read the morning *Atlanta Constitution* for the game account and the afternoon *Atlanta Journal* for in-depth coverage. There was no major league franchise in any sport below the Mason-Dixon line until the Atlanta

Braves arrived in 1966, and the Crackers occupied the pedestal.

We followed major league baseball, too. I read everything I could find about it in the daily papers and the monthly issues of *Sport* magazine that came in the mail. There would be an occasional glimpse of big league action in the newsreel at the picture show. But the Crackers dominated our hearts and minds. We saw them in person. We heard their voices as they chattered, "Hum baby, hum boy, hit to me." We recognized their gaits, the tilt of their caps. We saw the grounds crew relining the base paths after pre-game practice. We heard the umpire shout, "Play ball!"

The first time I saw a major league game in person I was perhaps twelve years old. We visited my sister and her husband in Ohio and went to Crosley Field to see the Cincinnati Reds play. But the main impression I took away from the game was that home plate was too far away from the grandstand; the diamond wasn't comfortably close to the fans as it was in Poncey. I wouldn't want to attend games there regularly, I decided.

MY FAVORITE BROADCASTER of Crackers games was Ernie Harwell. He was the voice of the Detroit Tigers for more than forty years, but to me he remains the voice of the Atlanta Crackers.

Harwell also is remembered as the only broadcaster ever traded for a player. Red Barber, the famous Brooklyn announcer, became seriously ill, and Branch Rickey, owner of the Dodgers, called Earl Mann, owner of the Crackers, and said he wanted Harwell as his broadcaster. But Harwell was under contract to Mann. So Rickey and Mann agreed that Harwell would be traded for Cliff Dapper, a catcher with Brooklyn's Class AAA farm team, Montreal. (The next year Dapper was promoted to player-manager of the Crackers.)

Wayne Holliday, Jimmy Lowe, Buck Manus, Chick Bragg and I huddled around the radio and eagerly bought into the illusion that Crackers announcers were on the scene at road games, though we knew better. Actually, they were in Atlanta, receiving bare-bones, pitch-by-pitch information from Western Union. They played canned crowd noises and hit wooden objects together to create the sound of bat on ball.

My favorite Cracker was Ralph Brown, a willowy center fielder. "The fleet Country Brown," as the Atlanta sportswriters called him, stole thirty-three bases in 1948. He was playing baseball in the Air Force when a teammate gave him his nickname. The fellow asked where he was from, and when Brown told him his home was Summerville, Georgia, the other player said he'd never heard of it, but it must be far out in the country.

It used to be said that every American boy dreams of playing in the major leagues. I didn't. I dreamed of playing for the Crackers and mastering the drag bunt, which was Country Brown's trademark. Brown, a left-handed hitter, was moving toward first base even before he deftly tapped the ball to a target that was out of reach of the first baseman, the pitcher, and the second baseman. I even vowed to overcome the handicap of being a right-handed batter.

Country Brown covered the outfield like a crop duster covers farmland. Fans even named the hill in Poncey's outfield "Brown Country." The problem came after he caught the ball. His arm was weak, or, as my daddy always said, "He couldn't break a window pane from six feet away." I suppose it was that liability that kept him out of the major leagues, but it didn't matter to me because I'd rather have him in Atlanta.

Many years later, when I was a sportswriter for the *Birmingham News,* I fulfilled a childhood dream by driving to Summerville and meeting Ralph Brown. I interviewed him for a feature story on a career minor leaguer. He was a judge, of all things. We had lunch in a meat-and-three cafe, topped it off with banana pudding, and it was obvious the townspeople knew who he was. They called him Ralph or Judge, not Country.

I enjoyed his stories, and he enjoyed telling them and hearing me speak unabashedly of my boyhood worship of him. "I made twelve hundred dollars a month, which was pretty good in those days," he told me. "During the season I lived in the Ponce de Leon Hotel, and I'd walk to the ballpark." Now, when I drive past the little hotel, I picture Country Brown strolling down Ponce de Leon Avenue, going to work.

Brown died on Christmas Eve of 1996. I still have a newspaper clipping in my desk drawer. It's datelined Rome, Georgia: "Ralph 'Country' Brown, one of the most popular players for the old Atlanta Crackers baseball team, died Tuesday following a long illness. He was 75.

"Brown was serving as chief magistrate judge in Chattooga County at the time of his death. He played minor league baseball for 12 years . . . Besides Atlanta, he also played for teams in Chattanooga, Little Rock, Birmingham, Nashville, and Louisville, where he retired."

PONCE DE LEON Park was quirky, to say the least.

Three tiers of advertising signs sat atop a long storage shed and formed the right field fence. The assemblage must have been fifty feet high, but a ball that cleared any tier was a home run. The distance down the line was 321 feet.

An abrupt hill rose behind the signs, and it was topped by a railroad track. Sometimes the engineer would blow his whistle at the crowd, and sometimes he would stop and watch the game. Bob Montag once hit a home run into a coal car. The car was 450 feet away, but it became known as the 518-mile homer. The ball traveled to Nashville and back to Atlanta, and the train's fireman got Montag to autograph it.

Center field was open, no fence. The steep hill was covered with kudzu and dotted by a magnolia tree. Only two men are verified to have hit balls into the magnolia. Babe Ruth did it in an exhibition game, and Crackers third baseman Eddie Mathews did it in a regular season game.

There were bleachers in left field, but the distance down the foul line was 365 feet. Finally, Earl Mann stretched a goofy two-foot-high hedge and fence across the area to give right-handed power hitters a break. Sometimes outfielders caught the ball only to fall over the fence, making the hit a home run.

I pulled for Earl Wooten, Davey Williams, Gene Verble, Norman Brown, Bob Thorpe, Ellis Clary, Ebba St. Claire, Dick Hoover, Art Fowler, Jack Dittmer, Chuck Tanner, the entire box of Crackers, but the only one who ever rivaled Country Brown as my idol was Eddie Mathews. During the pennant-winning season of 1950 he batted .286, hit thirty-two home runs and drove in 106 runs—and he was just eighteen years old.

Stardom in the minors doesn't necessarily translate into a major league career (Country Brown was proof of that), but Mathews played in the bigs seventeen years, hit 512 home runs, and reached the Baseball Hall of Fame. He was the only man to play with the Braves in Boston, Milwaukee, and Atlanta. He also managed the Atlanta Braves for three years. He was the real deal when he was a teenaged Cracker.

Mathews hit titanic homers in the minors and the majors. In addition to the magnolia tree shot in Poncey, he hit one that cleared the center field fence in Memphis, one that Country Brown reckoned traveled between five hundred and six hundred feet. Brown was on first base, and he halted to watch the ball. Manager Dixie Walker reprimanded him. "Don't ever stop like that again," Walker said.

"I won't," Brown answered, "until somebody hits another home run like that one."

The other teams of the Southern Association were the Birmingham Barons, the Memphis Chicks, the Nashville Vols, the Little Rock Travelers, the Chattanooga Lookouts, the Mobile Bears, and the New Orleans Pelicans. The one I really loved to hate was Nashville.

The Vols played in a strange ballpark called Sulphur Dell. It was widely suspected that the distance down the right field line was less than the minimum of 250 feet required by the rules. There was a tall fence, but Nashville stacked its lineup with left-handed batters who could hit massive pop-ups.

The 1948 Vols hit 183 home runs to obliterate the old Southern Association record of 157. The 1949 league champions featured catcher Carl Sawatski (.360 batting average, 45 homers, 153 runs batted in), outfielder Babe Barna (.341 BA, 42 HR, 139 RBI) and first baseman Tookie Gilbert (.334 BA, 33 HR, 122 RBI). Of course, all three were left-handed hitters. I just thought that was dirty pool, freaks playing in a freak stadium. "Let's see what you can do in a real ballpark!" I'd yell when the Vols come to Poncey.

When I saw the name Joe Engel in a headline in one of the Atlanta papers I eagerly read the story. "I live every day like it's New Year's Eve," the owner of the Chattanooga Lookouts said, and that's why he was the most colorful executive in the Southern Association. He was known as the Barnum of the Bush Leagues.

Engel once swapped shortstop Johnny Jones to Charlotte of the Sally League for a twenty-five pound turkey. He then invited sportswriters to a turkey dinner and proclaimed that he got the worst of the deal because "that was a mighty tough turkey." He traded another player to a Pacific Coast League team for a case of grapefruit, but I don't remember his commenting on the quality of the citrus.

One afternoon the umps called a game because of darkness. Engel figured there was enough daylight, and he wired the league president: "Suggest a rule be passed no umpires can have dates until 9 P.M." Engel provided copies of the telegram to the newspaper guys, of course, and it is said one umpire tried in vain for the longest to convince his wife it was just another of Joe's nutty jokes. Earl Mann, the owner of the Crackers, once arranged for a pile of horse manure to be dumped in Engel's front yard. It isn't difficult to decode that symbolic message.

I had been attending Crackers games since we lived in Tucker, a suburb of Atlanta. It was a short distance, and we'd go on the spur of the moment. We saw lots of games, and I had explored every inch of Poncey, above and below the stands. When Wayne Holliday and Jimmy Lowe would accompany my parents and me from Statham I would delight in introducing them to the possibilities of seeing more than a ball game.

I had once come fact to face with a pitcher named Shelby Kinney behind the first base grandstand, so I took them there, in hopes of seeing another Cracker. I showed them a ramp that led to the press box and said maybe we could catch a glimpse of an Atlanta sportswriter, maybe Ed Danforth, the sports editor of the *Journal*. I knew Earl Mann by sight, and I pointed him out as he toured the stands, chatting with fans. I knew about one section of bleachers where slippery sportsmen passed whiskey bottles around and made bets on whether the next batter would foul a ball, whether the next pitch would be a strike, whether the runner on first base would die in a double play. When a cop walked by they'd hide the evidence and sprout halos.

"Oh, yeah, I remember when Wayne and me used to go with you," Jimmy Lowe recalled one day in 2007. Then he made me jealous. "Do you remember Country Brown? I've got a program autographed by him and a program autographed by Eddie Mathews."

Under the third base stands was a booth with a blue neon sign, and it dispensed to me the first soft ice cream—the Dairy Queen type—that I ever ate. I didn't know such a treat existed, and that was the only place I could find it. After that, I never saw a game in that ballpark without an ice cream, and between innings I proudly led Wayne and Jimmy to that delicacy.

Sometimes my cousin, Jackie Wilson, who lived in Williamston, South Carolina, would visit us, and off we'd go to see the Crackers. When I visited Jackie we'd see the Anderson Rebels, who played in a Class B league. We didn't care about class—it was professional baseball.

Jackie was younger than me, and one day my mother gave him some of my clothes. He particularly admired a long-sleeved flannel shirt, and nothing would suit him but that he wear that shirt to Poncey on a steamy July evening.

Maybe I knew every square inch of Poncey, but like most of the citizenry I was naïve about golf, which was still considered by most folks a rich person's sport. Louise Suggs, the famous pro, performed exhibitions before Crackers games, and I was astounded that she could hit a golf ball farther than Eddie Mathews could hit a baseball. She knocked them over the center field magnolia, over the right field signs, over the left field bleachers. Louise's father, Johnny Suggs, had been a Cracker. He pitched a no-hitter in 1921.

PONCE DE LEON Park was my field of dreams, but soon nightmares intruded. Television sets became commonplace in American homes, and more and more folks were acquiring air conditioning. That combination made staying at the house more attractive than sweating at the ballpark. Why, major league games were being played right there on a screen in the living room while the family members balanced TV dinners on their knees. There had been fifty-nine minor leagues in 1949, but by 1963 the total had plummeted to eighteen.

The Southen Association died in 1961; only 59,000 came to Poncey that year. The Crackers joined the International League—and played their final season, 1965, not in Poncey but in the new Atlanta stadium the Braves took over in 1966.

During their lifetime (1920–65) the Crackers won more league championships, eighteen, than any other team in baseball except the New York Yankees.

Poncey was doomed, of course. The park and some adjacent land were auctioned on October 25, 1965, for $1,250,000. Before the sale began the auctioneer asked organist Dale Stone to play "Take Me Out to the Ballgame" because "Earl Mann says he wants to hear it one more time in the ballpark."

Then came the wrecking ball. I drove along Ponce de Leon Avenue one day during the demolition and stopped and stole a green slat off the back of a grandstand seat for a souvenir. I still have it.

Earl Mann died in 1990, and his ashes were spread under the magnolia tree in center field. Last time I looked, the tree was still there, gazing down on stores instead of a ballpark.

Chapter 5

When I was a kid in Statham the green of springtime was neon, as vivid as the pictures on the plasma TVs of today. Fall winds chased multiple shades of brown and tan and gray across the rippling field of broomsedge that grew beside our house. The breasts of the bream I caught in Rozzie's Pond were as golden as anything in Tut's tomb. The pomegranates from the tree near the school were so distinctly sour-sweet that I felt I was at a potentate's table.

Our senses are poised for action when we're young. We see and taste and smell and touch like we never will again. But we don't know we never will again. Our senses dim, and the objects of our senses lose their savor. The struggle to pay our daily tariffs, to keep life right side up, renders them dimmer still. My God, I'd pay a ransom to smell a gardenia the way I used to smell a gardenia.

Nature gave our senses a workout in Statham. There was much to taste, much to smell, much to see, much to hear and feel.

I pull a honeysuckle bloom from the vine in my backyard in Alabama, bite off the end and suck, but what it yields today isn't the nectar that was offered by the little trumpet flowers in Georgia. The clear drop of liquid isn't there; I know it was there in Statham.

Wild plums grew beside dirt roads, and we slammed on the brakes and skidded our bikes to a stop and wiped the dust off each plum and filled our pockets with prizes that have never been duplicated in my life since.

The pine thicket beside Perry's Pond dripped resin that captured bugs and then preserved their little corpses, and the piney woods fragrance cleared our nostrils like the thrust of a green knife.

The barbecue we bought at the black men's baseball games in a pasture outside of town was the most succulent I have ever tasted. It was prepared with the all-night patience that separates real barbecue from the imitation stuff that dominates today. A sandwich consisted of not two but three pieces of loaf bread with generous helpings of pork between the slices. It cost a quarter.

The cotton fields were dusted with an insecticide named Toxaphene, and though it burned our eyes we appreciated its acrid ubiquitousness because cotton was still king, and by picking it we could make money and attend the Southeastern Fair in Atlanta. I ride through the countryside today and not only smell no Toxaphene but see no cotton. I wish I could experience the pungent poison again.

The bright red shirts and silver britches and silver helmets of the Georgia Bulldogs dazzled me. Those britches weren't gray, as Georgia's later became, they really were silver. Satin, I suppose. I can picture them now, but I don't remember who wore the white jerseys and who wore the colored ones in the last football game I saw.

Salted peanuts came in little cellophane packs, and I used to cup my hand around the mouth of an RC Cola bottle and pour the nuts in. They created a fizz that sometimes overflowed, and I delighted in the taste of the two very different entities. The other day I bought some salted peanuts and poured them into a soft drink can—but whatever magic the recipe had created in 1949 had vanished.

I remember the threshing sound of my bicycle as it navigated the roads of Statham. The rear end made a noise like a man with a scythe in a wheat field, but it ran fine. I remember the sound of that bike after more than half a century, but a few minutes ago I tried to remember the sound of the car I drove this morning and I couldn't.

I recall the pent-up dusty smell of the Statham High gymnasium A pickup game of basketball left your hands black and slick. You had to spit on them and then wipe your hands on your shirt to control the ball. Where did the dust come from and why was there so much of it? I don't know. The floor was unvarnished, so perhaps the dust clung more tenaciously than it would have on a slicker surface.

We smoked rabbit tobacco, at least the boys did. It was a dry, gray weed that grew wild and plentifully in the fields around Statham. We shredded the leaves from the stalk and wrapped them in newspaper, licked the paper to make it stick, touched a match to the cigarette (and blew out the fire that inevitably resulted) and puffed away. I remember the unique taste. I don't smoke anything, but a few months ago I spotted some rabbit tobacco—the first I'd seen in years—and took it home and lit up, just for the heck of it. All I tasted was burning newspaper, and I tossed it in the fireplace.

The popcorn that sold for a nickel in the Royal Theater in Statham was popped right before your eyes. The white morsels did their antic dance in a glass-enclosed machine, and the aroma was the royalty of smells. You ordered it buttered and salted to your taste, my friend. Now I toss a bag in the microwave and hope it will taste and smell like that from the picture show, but it never does.

WE HELD HANDS with our sweethearts in the picture show, and what a sensory thrill that was to an adolescent. But that ritual didn't begin until after we'd eaten the popcorn. Securing the box between your knees, eating popcorn with one hand and holding your girl's hand with the other while she did the same would have been a breach of our etiquette, even if Emily Post never thought of it. Occasionally I'd dump the last third of a box just to get on with the handholding.

I described the rite in my novel *Water Oaks*. Chuck Ridley and Becky Roberts are the sweethearts. (Incidentally, Lucky was a Bingo-type game conducted every Wednesday night at the Royal Theater by my grandmother's brother, Embre McDonald, the projectionist.)

From the corner of his eye Chuck saw Becky's left hand, loose on her knee. He slipped his right hand under it, their fingers entwined, and he rested his elbow and forearm on her arm support, her arm lying on his. He squeezed her fingers; she returned the squeeze.

The ritual. Holding hands in the show. Prelude to . . . nothing. The beginning and end of the night's courtship. Transmitting and transmuting. The delicious voltage from her damp palm, slim fingers, rounded knuckles, and smooth nails agitating his nerve endings; the base metal of a blue-jeaned, pimpled, fuzz-lipped boy being alchemized into the warm gold of the fondly touched.

He knew they would hold hands until the last monster died (as on other nights they had held hands until the last cowboy had ridden into the horizon, the last plane had touched down on the carrier deck), though his arm would go to sleep and his fingers would stiffen and hurt and, he supposed, hers would, too, but they would be sorry when it was time for Errol to flash on the ceiling lights. The Lucky game on stage, which elicited anticipatory murmurs from the grown-ups, would be anticlimactic for them. He looked at his girl in the darkness, at the shoulder-length brown, almost black, hair and brown eyes that reflected the flickers of the screen, at the delicate nose, at the pearliness of teeth between her barely parted, thin lips, at the rounded silhouette of the front of her blouse. He ached in his knees and in his shoulders, and he was afraid he would lose his breath. He hoped Becky didn't notice a shiver.

Gayle Mobley was my first sweetheart in Statham, and Harriette Robertson was my second and last one. The faint traces of salt and butter on our hands did nothing to lessen the thrill of holding hands. Might even have increased it.

When we moved to Statham in 1948 we put some of our stuff in an empty back room in the depot. I was sifting through the treasures I had accumulated in my twelve years, and I came across my Captain Midnight binoculars, little plastic things that were black so as not to catch the eye of a Nazi sniper.

Gayle's parents had a grocery store at the corner of Railroad and Jefferson streets, just across from the depot. I raised the binoculars and watched their daughter for a couple of minutes. I think it was the first time I ever saw her. She was a cute little thing, and I wanted to get to know her, so I made a point of doing exactly that. (It wasn't until 2006 that I told her about the binoculars.)

Gayle was petite. She was four-feet-eleven. But she was a firebrand basketball player who made the girls' rules of that time seem as ridiculous as they truly were. A girl couldn't run the length of the court as a boy could, the lawgivers decreed from on high, so each team was allowed three forwards and three guards with no player permitted to cross the center line. The forwards played only offense, the guards only defense. Nonsense. Gayle, who was a forward, could have run all day.

I'm not sure of the origin, but Gayle had a signature line: "What's it to you?" She didn't have to be angry. She just said it. I still have a valentine with "What's it to you?" written on the back.

Gayle helped out in her parents' place of business. It was a grocery store and meat market, but they also sold cloth for dresses. Women would rummage through the bolts of cloth and leave things in a mess. Gayle would restore order and silently complain that they did the same thing with the same cloth a few days before.

Gayle's job was to have supper on the table at the end of the day, but she found time to bounce around with our little gang and to shoot basketball at the goal in her yard. She was as vibrant as a bowstring, a fascinating girl who animated everyone in her presence.

I DON'T REMEMBER why Gayle Mobley and I stopped being sweethearts or how Harriette Robertson and I became sweethearts. I do recall there was a blip in the second process. Wayne Holliday, my best friend, and I both claimed Harriette as our girlfriend. Obviously she liked us both, for she sat between Wayne and me in the Royal Theater—and held hands with both of us. Yep, at the same time.

I beat Wayne's time (now there's a quaint phrase) with Harriette, but he found the love of his life right there in our school. Carolyn Deaton, who lived on a farm outside town, became his sweetheart and then, in 1956, his wife. She never considered remarrying after Wayne died in 1978. "Wayne was the only guy I ever dated," she told me. "He was the only one I ever loved."

They say opposites attract. Harriette and I couldn't have been more opposite in the matter of bicycles. Her bike was a gem. It was blue, no dents, and since there was a basket mounted over the front fender she was always nominated to go to the grocery store to get the fixings for our weenie roasts. She took care of her bicycle, and it was always clean, even the tires.

My bike, on the other hand, was stripped for speed. My cronies and I raced through what the Indy 500 announcer called "the deadly north turn" of Indianapolis Motor Speedway (indicated by the street light in front of my house on Broad Street). There were no fenders on my bicycle, no handlebar grips, no chain guard. To the consternation of my mother, the sprocket occasionally ate the legs of my blue jeans. Some of the rips she could mend, some she couldn't, in which case I wore them ragged. If the bike's rear end slipped I poured in kerosene (at ten cents a gallon) and it stopped.

Harriette was a dark, willowy beauty who also played basketball. "I'll say this for you," Daddy told me, "you've got the prettiest girl in Statham." I told her that many years later, and she was pleased. I could always remember her birthday. I was born on August 31, 1936, and she was born the next day, September 1, 1936. It's quite convenient that Sandra Bolton, the woman I've been married to for the last fifty-five years, also was born on September 1, 1936.

Our little gang had our weenie roasts in the dirt road in front of Harriette's house at night, the flames casting our shadows on Elizabeth Street. We were impatient, and if the sticks we'd rounded up happened to be wet, we'd roast the weenies in the blaze from newspapers. So what if they weren't done? Harriette's mother would step outside and deliver the standard lecture that we should be careful and not allow the fire to spread and burn down the town. We would play walking games, and Harriette and I would stroll in the dark cemetery a block away, smooching (do people still use that word?) in the company of the pioneers of Statham and the dear departed of later years.

(In 1993 I sat on a brick wall under a magnolia tree in that cemetery and planned my novel, *The Lost Sunshine*. I was pleasantly surprised that it came to me so clearly and quickly. I completed the outline in an hour.)

Funny what embarrasses kids. Funny what you remember. The youngsters of Statham rode the school bus to the Southeastern Fair in Atlanta and returned late in the night. Harriette and I hit the carny game booths and cotton candy stand and the freak show and the funhouse and the Joie Chitwood Hell Drivers auto thrill show and the Whip and the Ferris wheel and the Bullet and the best of all, the Greyhound, the wooden roller coaster that would later be destroyed in a scene from the movie *Smokey and the Bandit II*. My nickname was Bunny because of the aforementioned white hair I had as a little boy, and I stopped at a souvenir stand and bought a silly straw sombrero and asked the man to spray-paint "Bunny" on the upturned brim.

He did, and he handed the thing to Harriette and said, "Here's your hat, Bunny." She said, "Oh, it's not mine," and passed it to me.

No big deal? Well, it was to me. We'd paid our own ways on the rides and in the booths and in the shows, but an adult obviously believed I was buying a souvenir of the fair for my girl—obviously believed I indeed should have been buying a souvenir of the fair for my girl. But I wasn't. I was buying it for myself. I was embarrassed, and I felt selfish. I never enjoyed that hat after that, never even wore it. I burned it in a fire Daddy had started to get rid of some household junk.

We kids made money for the fair by picking cotton. At the end of my first day I proudly dragged my sack of what I knew was at least one hundred pounds of cotton to the scales. "Twenty-seven pounds," the man said. I learned that laughing and kidding with your friends and throwing dirt clods at them doesn't mix with cotton picking. I picked a few days more but never came close to one hundred pounds. It's hard not to laugh and kid with your friends and throw clods at them when they're right there beside you.

Harriette was still my sweetheart when we moved from Statham to Winder in 1951. The distance was just eight miles, but when you're too young for a driver's license it might as well be 1,008 miles.

We renewed our friendship years later when we both were married and had children. I was on my way to Athens to cover a football game for the *Birmingham News*, and I stopped at her home in Statham. I went to a school dance with her and her husband at the gymnasium that night. I think they were chaperones. Harriette worked at the Barrow County Board of Education office in Winder, and after that I'd occasionally drop by her office and we'd laugh about the old days. She kept me up to date on what was happening in Statham, who had died and who was about to.

Harriette married Bobby Young, an older man we kids had admired as a uniformed member of the U. S. Navy. Years later my boyhood image of Bobby majestically sailing the seas was altered when he told me he was seasick the entire time he was on a ship and lost an alarming amount of weight.

Harriette and Bobby and Sandra and I vacationed together a couple of times. Once I took a newly purchased book about all the edible plants that grow in the wild (people who are lost in the woods frequently starve though they are surrounded by food, it said) and tried to cook some weeds. Sandra boiled them for an hour, but they were too tough to eat. I asked her to keep boiling, because the book assured they were tasty. She boiled them another hour, but they were too tough to eat. A few more minutes should do it, I told Sandra, with no trace of confidence in my voice. After three hours they were still too tough to eat, and everyone had a good laugh when I dumped the mess behind our mountain cabin.

We went to Alpine Helen and waded in the Chattahoochee River. Every Georgia school kid used to memorize Sidney Lanier's "Song of the Chattahoochee," a poem about duty, and standing in the perfectly clear stream I felt special. We fished for trout. I had dug a can of worms at home, but we weren't having any success with them. A native asked me what we were using for bait, and when I told him, he said, "You can't catch trout with worms. You have to use little niblet corn." So I freed the worms and went to the grocery store and bought a can of corn. Still no luck. Another native asked me what we were using for bait, and when I told him he said, "You can't catch trout with corn. You have to use worms."

We didn't catch trout, but Sandra hooked a water moccasin, jerked it onto the bank, threw her rod down and ran, leaving the cutting of the line and retrieving of the tackle to me.

Bobby Young said that trip to Helen was the most fun he'd had in his life. I was pleased. It's nice to know you're part of the most fun someone had in his life.

Bobby died of heart failure, and Harriette married Robert Nowell, a widower. I never got to know him as well as I did Bobby, but he was a cordial fellow, and I liked him.

One day I received a shocking phone call from Harriette's family. A heart problem had sent her into a coma. She wasted away for several months, and then she died. She was just sixty years old.

Wayne Holliday was gone, Rose Marie Herrin was gone, and Harriette Robertson was gone. Time had taken a cruel, premature toll on our little gang. Ten years later, on Tuesday, January 16, 2007, I dialed Buck Manus's phone number in Cookeville, Tennessee. I was going to tell him I was writing this book, and I wanted to hear his memories of our years together in Statham. His wife, Paula, answered, and I asked to speak to him. "Buck died Friday," she said. I was stunned.

He had told her all the old Statham stories. "He had such fond memories of those days," Paula said. She grew up in a small town in Michigan, and she shared some of her stories with me. It was good to be a small-town boy in Georgia, and it was good to be a small-town girl in Michigan.

A year later, on January 29, 2008, my friend Becky Dunagan called. "I seem to be the Statham information center," she said. This piece of information was that Chick Bragg, who lived in Gulfport, Mississippi, had died.

So five of the nine members of our little gang are gone. How I'd like to see their eager, optimistic faces in the flickering light of a weenie roast one more time.

Chapter 6

Our frequent moves from town to town—and sometimes just from neighborhood to neighborhood—meant saying goodbye to buddies and sweethearts, but they did open new vistas of adventure. I faced each move with trepidation, but curiosity impelled me to scope out the area, to discover its opportunities. After all, I might be living there for six whole months (he said sardonically).

Our first home in Statham was a commonplace white frame house on Highway 29 that was perhaps a quarter-mile from the depot and the downtown businesses. We had actually owned a house in Tucker—two, in fact—but now we were renters again. Buck Holliday, the longtime mayor of Statham, was our landlord and next-door neighbor.

There was an open field of a few acres beside the house, and behind the field was a small wooded area with a slight stream. I was twelve years old and blessed with a keen imagination that was honed by being alone so much when I was making the transition from town to town. So I didn't need the Great Plains, a national forest, or the Mississippi River to enjoy the outdoors. The most commonplace plot of earth or a trickle of water became whatever I willed them to be.

My newfound friends, Wayne Holliday, Jimmy Lowe, Buck Manus, and Chick Bragg, were open to my invitations to "camp out" in the field. We spent the night under the stars, but we were impatient, eager to get on with it, so we pitched camp well before dark. We were settled in before the indigo sunset ended the day. In our minds we were soldiers hunkered down in a scarred battlefield. Or we were cowboys on the trail, weary from a day of driving our herd. Or we were pioneers, answering the call of Westward, Ho.

We built campfires, whether it was cold or hot, which probably wasn't a great idea, considering we were surrounded by brittle broomsedge. But what's a camp without a campfire? Besides, we kept the fires low and contained within a circle of rocks, and all we ever did was heat pork and beans in a frying pan. Our bedclothes were army surplus sleeping bags or family surplus tattered quilts. We stayed up half the night, laughing and replaying ball games, and then we slept the sleep of the weary just. When the morning sun and the clacking of transport trucks lumbering by woke us up, we trudged to my house where Mother and eggs and bacon and grits and toast were waiting.

My cousin Jackie Wilson, who would visit from his home in Williamston, South Carolina, and I still laugh about the time we "swam" across the quiet stream behind the field. It was perhaps four feet wide and ten inches deep, but we were pursuing villains of some stripe or other, and we shucked our clothes and forded the river. We got plenty muddy, but that was a small price to pay to keep Statham safe from the bad guys.

In front of my house, across Highway 29 and the railroad tracks, was a narrow strip of land that occasionally served Wayne, Jimmy, Buck, Chick, and me as a baseball field, sort of an auxiliary to the diamond at school. It wasn't adequate even for eleven-year-old and twelve-year-old batters, but we imagined balls clearing the low bank in left field and landing on the railroad tracks were balls clearing the signs in Ponce de Leon Park in Atlanta and landing on those railroad tracks.

Right field was a problem. There was a fenced-in garden beside a house, and a prodigious lick could send a ball over the chicken-wire fence. For a while the owner put up with us retrieving our baseballs, but his garden began to wear thin and so did his patience. He said that any ball that went over his fence stayed over his fence. Wayne was our only left-handed batter, so he was most likely to hit a ball into that garden—and least likely to defy the owner and trespass through the fence and get it back. We didn't have baseballs to spare, so the garden of forbidden horsehide fruit and the scant dimensions of the ball field caused us to bid it goodbye.

It was certainly convenient to Jimmy and me. It was about fifty yards from our homes. We laughed about it in a phone conversation the other day. "Y'all lived across the railroad," Jimmy said. "Do you remember that strip of land behind my house, beside the railroad, where we played baseball?"

"We obviously couldn't hit a ball very far," I said.

"Why, I could spit across that plot of land, it was so narrow," Jimmy reckoned.

THERE WAS A garage behind that first Statham house that had been used to store junk. Cousin Jackie and I were exploring the boxes when we came across three newborn rats. They hadn't even opened their eyes. We never saw their mother. We moved them inside the house and took it upon ourselves to give them milk with a medicine dropper. All we saw were cute little creatures and, as is typical of kids, we gave no thought to the future—what they would grow up to be, I mean.

Daddy did. "They're rats," he said after he discovered our pets. "You can't have rats in the house or even in the garage. For goodness sake, boys." He gave us the bubonic plague lecture, and when he was finished we didn't want to raise rats anymore. We didn't want to abandon them to starvation, though—so we executed them with our Red Ryder air rifles.

Every boy of that era had—or wanted—a Daisy Red Ryder air rifle. You've seen the wonderful movie, *A Christmas Story*, in which little Ralphie, played by Peter Billingsley, has his heart set on a BB gun? That's how it was with my generation. And, yep, we'd all heard the film's oft-repeated warning: "You'll shoot your eye out." (I later worked with a newspaperman who actually did shoot his eye out with a BB gun when he was a boy. Either that or another kid did it for him, I don't remember which.)

I loved Red Ryder movies. They were introduced by Red Ryder (Bill Elliott) and his Indian sidekick, Little Beaver (Robert Blake), stepping from the pages of a Red Ryder novel. Not only was that intro the cleverest thing I'd ever seen, but Little Beaver was just a boy, like me, and that hinted that in a crisis I could perform heroically, too. Shades of Robin, the Boy Wonder. Decades later when I watched on TV a frightened, white-haired Robert Blake who was accused of killing his wife, I was saddened that Little Beaver had come to such a pass.

The first Red Ryder BB gun I ever owned was a Christmas present from my parents when we lived in Tucker. I was as excited as Ralphie. But profound disappointment and confusion lurked just ahead. There was a leather thong attached to a ring on the rifle, and I slipped the thong over the handlebars of my bicycle and began riding. I was nearly to my daddy's depot when the barrel of the BB gun hung in the front wheel of the bike, jamming against the fork. The bicycle came to a sudden, complete stop, throwing me over the handlebars. I surveyed the damage and saw that I wasn't hurt, but some wheel spokes of the bike were broken—and the barrel of my new Red Ryder BB gun was seriously bent and scarred.

I went to the depot, told Daddy what happened, and showed him the damage. He remembered that I had said something about a gun that would shoot around corners, and he accused me of bending the barrel on purpose, trying to make it shoot around corners. He added that he would give me a whipping when he got home that afternoon. He seemed as frustrated as he was angry. I was dumbfounded, not to mention frightened. I couldn't believe he really thought I'd bend my new prize air rifle on purpose. And Daddy had never given me a whipping, not once. I was facing the unknown, which was scary.

It turned out that he never would give me a whipping, not once. He had cooled off when he got home, and he said he knew it was an accident, he was sorry he had reacted badly, and he was sorry my new BB gun was ruined. Later Mother explained that we were stressed for money, and buying the air rifle had been a strain, and that was why this even-tempered man had so uncharacteristically lost his temper.

The BB gun would still shoot, but not straight. Under the circumstances, I couldn't enjoy it. But one person's trash is another person's treasure, and I sold the damaged air rifle for a dollar to a boy who didn't have one, and he prized it. We took that buck, and Daddy somehow came up with some more money, and he bought me a new replacement Red Ryder BB gun that he couldn't afford. It went with me from Tucker to Statham.

Air rifles afford myriad opportunities for mischief, but if any of our little gang in Statham ever misused a BB gun—with the dramatic exception of sore loser Buck Manus shooting Gayle Mobley because her football team beat his—I don't remember it. We never shot out a streetlight, never shot out a window, never shot a dog. That's something to be proud of. Now, in Tucker we had air rifle battles, with a rule that a warrior could not aim above the waist. I can testify that a BB striking the anklebone full force does smart.

I DID MAKE mischief one night in Statham, and more than a half-century later I look back on the act and wonder why I did it because it was not characteristic of me. I was walking home alone one night from the picture show, and I passed a house that was freshly painted. The paint was still wet, and I threw several handfuls of dirt against a wall, making a significant mess.

A day or two later I was riding with my parents, and when we passed the house Daddy said the owner had told him about the incident. He didn't know who the perpetrator was. "I can't understand anybody doing something that sorry," Daddy said. "That's just low-down behavior." That stung. I had an overactive conscience anyway, and that remark pierced it to the core. We stopped at a store and Daddy went inside while Mother and I waited in the car. "That was me that threw the dirt on the house," I told her.

It was a bad thing to do, she said, and she was disappointed in me. But she assured me I was not a bad person. "Do you think I should tell Daddy?" I asked. "No," she said. His record of never having whipped me might have ended if I had. That would have been justice, for it was, as Daddy said, a sorry thing to do, low-down behavior.

I remember another piece of mischief that didn't hurt anyone—unless you count being scared to death as getting hurt.

It was picture day at Statham High. The photographer was shooting individual snapshots, and a covey of ninth-grade girls waited by the stage in the auditorium. I spotted a green snake on the campus, and I plucked the wiggly thing off its observation post on the limb of a tree, concealed it under my shirt, and bounced into the schoolhouse. I wrapped the snake around my neck, stuck its head in my mouth, and silently approached the girls. They stared quizzically. Was it a green rope? A green ribbon? Why did he have it in his mouth? What was it?

When I was in their midst I popped the snake's head out of my mouth. Their shrieks could have been heard in Atlanta as they fled from the auditorium.

The joke did not endear me to the girls, the photographer, or Paul Barrett, the principal, but nothing came of it. Mr. Barrett loved a good story, and he wasn't about to make a capital case of something that would be told and retold for decades.

Mr. Barrett was a central figure in another piece of mischief that I observed. He demonstrated something akin to the wisdom of Solomon, with a dollop of humor. We were between classes when Mrs. Evelyn Harris, a teacher, glanced out her classroom window and saw that Stanley Pentecost was letting the air out of one of the tires on her car. She was upset, and she sent out an SOS to Mr. Barrett, who came to her room. Stanley had deflated one tire and started on another, and the frantic teacher pled, "Stop him, Mr. Barrett!"

"Just wait," Mr. Barrett said.

We watched Stanley deflate all four tires. When he had finished Mr. Barrett confronted him, calmly ordering, "Stanley, go down to the filling station and borrow a hand pump and an air gauge and come back and pump up all four of these tires." I'd say the punishment fit the crime. Indeed, the punishment exactly paralleled the crime.

OVER THE DECADES I had watched our old house on Highway 29 fall on hard times. It had become an eyesore. So I was pleased one day in 2006 when I noticed it was being renovated and transformed from a ramshackle residence into a veterinarian's office. I explained to the receptionist that I had lived there and asked if I might have a look-see. I gazed fondly at a sitting room on the east side of the house where Mother and I had listened to the radio broadcasts of the 1948 World Series.

Mother was a baseball fan—she watched the Atlanta Braves on TV until she died, never missing a game. At twelve years old I had become acutely aware of sports, and I followed the University of Georgia football team and the Atlanta Crackers baseball team—two that I could practically reach out and touch—but I kept up with the big leagues, too, through the *Atlanta Journal* and my subscription to *Sport* magazine. My favorite big league baseball team was the Cleveland Indians, and the Tribe (as the sportswriters called the Indians) was in the World Series against the Boston Braves. As icing on the cake, my favorite big league player was Cleveland's Lou Boudreau.

The close of the 1948 season had dripped with drama. After 154 games, Cleveland and the Boston Red Sox had finished in a tie for first place. Never before in American League history had that happened. So there was a playoff game—and Boudreau hit two home runs in an 8-3 Indians victory. I was delighted.

Boudreau not only was the shortstop, he was the manager. His movie star good looks made him one of the most identifiable athletes in the country. He batted .355, second only to Ted Williams's .369 in the American League, and he was voted the Most Valuable Player. When I wasn't pretending I was Lou Boudreau, I was pretending I was Bob Feller, the pitcher with the ominous windup that preceded the delivery of an invisible fast ball. Feller won nineteen games and Gene Bearden and Bob Lemon won twenty for the Indians that season. Cleveland was loaded with pitchers.

I couldn't hate the Boston Braves, though. It was their first National League pennant since 1914, and their shortstop was a good old Southern boy, a former LSU football player named Alvin Dark, who had hit .322 in his first full season in the majors. Warren Spahn and Johnny Sain were the ace pitchers, but there was a dropoff after them, prompting the Braves' supposed pitching strategy: "Spahn then Sain—then pray for rain."

Mother and I ate her scrumptious half-moon apple pies and drank hot chocolate and bemoaned the injustice of the world as Feller pitched a two-hitter in the opener but lost to Sain 1-0. Phil Masi scored the run, though the Indians were certain he had been picked off at second base. I was sure he had been picked off, too, because I knew Boudreau wouldn't argue unless he was right. But the umpire disagreed with the Indians and with me.

But in the end justice triumphed. The Indians won the next four games, and surely Cleveland and Lou Boudreau would reign over the major leagues forever.

A repeated observation in this tome is that it's strange how the human mind works, how we recall the insignificant and forget the important. I remember my great-aunt, Lorna McDonald, coming to visit during the broadcast of one of the 1948 World Series games. She probably didn't know which teams were in the World Series, or maybe that there was any such thing as a World Series. Mother, ever the mannered lady, turned off the radio and entertained Lorna for an hour without a trace of impatience. When Lorna left, Mother said, "I thought she'd stay all day. Turn that radio back on."

There's a postscript to that 1948 World Series. When I was a sportswriter with the *Birmingham News*, Bob Feller came to town for a baseball card show. He was aging, and he wore thick eyeglasses. I made arrangements to interview him in his hotel room and he was impressed by my knowledge of the 1948 Indians and the World Series. I wrote a feature story about him, and I was surprised to receive a letter from Feller a few days later. He thanked me for the story and noted that it was accurate, a quality that wasn't always present in the stories that had been written about him over the years.

I thought that was so neat, that Bob Feller, one of the most celebrated baseball players in history, the subject of thousands of stories during his amazing career, would take the time to write a thank-you note to a sportswriter in backwater Birmingham, Alabama.

And I still think Phil Masi was out.

NUMEROUS ATHLETES I had known only by radio and newspaper became flesh and blood to me after I became a sportswriter. It was as though a boy's wish had come true even though he had never thought to wish it.

I became enamored of the 1950 Philadelphia Phillies. It was a young squad known as the Whiz Kids. I loved the nickname, and I loved the red-pinstriped uniforms they wore as a counterpoint to the New York Yankees' black pinstripes. They even had red caps. My favorite Phillies were Richie Ashburn, the dashing blond center fielder, and Robin Roberts, the twenty-game-winning pitcher. I said if I ever had a son I would name him Robin (which I did not do, by the way). There was a full-page composite color picture of some of the Whiz Kids in *Sport* magazine, and I cut it out and taped it on my bedroom wall along with numerous other color portraits from the magazine. (Many years later I bought a stack of *Sport* magazines from the 1950s in an antique store. The color pictures had been clipped out of them, too, and no doubt taped to some other boy's wall.)

Later, Bubba Church, a Birmingham resident who was a pitcher for the 1950 Phillies, and I became friends. When Bubba was inducted into the Alabama Sports Hall of Fame in 2000 he phoned me and said, "Robin Roberts is coming to town for the induction. He wants to play a round of golf, but I just don't have the time. Would you play with him?"

Would I? If a genie had told me in 1950 that I would be playing golf with Robin Roberts fifty years hence, I probably would have dropped dead on the spot.

I've never played a more delightful round of golf. Roberts was energetic and a wonderful conversationalist. He told a story on Church. "We played a doubleheader against the Cubs, and Bubba pitched a three-hit shutout in the first game. Then I pitched a two-hit shutout in the second one. Bubba said, 'How could you do that to me? I was going to be all over the newspapers with my three-hitter, and you come along and pitch a two-hitter.'"

I soon realized how Church felt. I parred the first hole at Birmingham's Highland Park, but Roberts birdied it. He shot 74, one more stroke than his age.

"Nothing has changed more than how they regard pitching in the big leagues," Roberts told me. "They use eleven-man staffs and have setup men and closers. Very few of us would leave the game unless we got knocked around." He remembered when Brooklyn's Don Newcombe tried to pitch a doubleheader against the Phillies in the stretch in 1950. "He beat us in the first game and was behind 2-0 when he left for a pinch hitter in the seventh inning of the second game."

There was a melancholy note to our day, though. Roberts reeled off a long list of Whiz Kids who had left this mortal coil, among them Richie Ashburn, Del Ennis, Eddie Waitkus, Blix Donnelly, Puddinhead Jones, Granny Hamner, Jim Konstanty, Bill Nicholson, and Ken Silvestri. My fiend Bubba Church joined them in 2001, the year after his induction into the Alabama Sports Hall of Fame. Life is, indeed, a terminal illness.

Chapter 7

"It takes a heap o' livin' in a house t' make it home," poet Edgar Guest reckoned in the copy of *One Hundred and One Famous Poems* that I had in the eighth grade at Statham (and still have).

Not really, not such a heap. We lived in a house on Broad Street just two years and four months, but of all the dwellings that I grew up in, it's the one that smiles back at me when I ride past it on my visits to Statham. It's the one I think of as my boyhood home, though I had enough homes for a dozen boyhoods.

Maybe it's home because it's where I was living when we left Statham in 1951, when I was fifteen years old. It was the last outpost for those magic days before I crept off to a dreary existence in Winder.

I've been inside the house one time since 1951. I was walking along Broad Street several years ago, and the owner of the home, Larry Savage, was working in the yard. I stopped and chatted with him and told him I used to live there. "Would you like to see inside?" he asked. It was a kind offer, one I accepted with pleasure. He guided me through the old place, and the most striking aspect was that my bedroom seemed much smaller than I had remembered it being. Why does everything shrink when we become adults?

The word "move" generally created knots in my stomach, but I was delighted with the move from the house on Highway 29 to the one on Broad Street. The school, the stores, the cafe, the depot, the picture show, my friends' homes—everything necessary to my daily functioning—was on the opposite side of Highway 29 from me. To get there I had to carefully push my bike across a busy highway and then ride it on the crossties between the railroad rails, always watching and listening for trains. Now, from Broad Street, everything was within easy reach.

I still have a copy of the deed for that seven-room, one-story wooden house. My daddy bought if from Mrs. Mary Turner Jenkins for $2,000. There were to be ninety-six monthly payments of $25.32. The deed is dated June 2, 1949.

It was already an old house. It rested on brick pillars. Daddy and I bricked up between them ourselves to keep the wind from dancing under the floors during the winter. He laid the brick and I mixed the cement and hauled the bricks and refilled the water bottle. There was a spacious front porch and a small back porch with a well that was no longer needed.

The front yard wasn't large, wasn't small, just ordinary, with a couple of pecan trees and a privet hedge that separated the yard from the dirt sidewalk, but the backyard was expansive. We had a pigpen across the back of the property with two or three hogs. One day Daddy found me at my Aunt Eva Smith's house and said, "Leave your bicycle and get in the car and come home with me. The sow is having pigs."

We rushed home and for the first time I witnessed the miracle of birth. I recall the piglets came wrapped in something that looked like cellophane. Daddy helped remove them from their packaging while their suspicious mamma grunted.

I remember one of our hogs catching a snake in the pen one sunny morning. She shook it like a piece of rope and finally ate it. Fair's fair, because we ate the pigs. That's why we raised them. A black man slaughtered them and prepared the meat for a share of it. My job was to hose out the contents of the intestines and turn them into chitterlings—which, of course, everyone called chitlins. The smell was awful during the hosing and later during the cooking, but I liked them and still do. My wife, Sandra, normally an adventurous chef, cooked chitlins for me one time, fifty years ago, and vowed never again.

I ALWAYS THOUGHT of us as farmers without a farm. In our backyard on a busy street in Atlanta, Daddy raised chickens for frying. In our backyard in Tucker he raised fine bantams such as Dominiques, Millefleurs, and Cochins to sell (Bolton's Bantam Yard, read the sign the Purina chicken feed company gave us). We had the hogs and raised vegetables in the backyard in Statham. Daddy subscribed to the *Progressive Farmer* magazine and actually read the articles. He could talk farming with the rurals who hung around his depots and the various country stores. All that was missing was a farm. Thank God!

Someone had a calf for sale, and Daddy said I could have it if I wanted it. Of course I wanted it. We would put it in a shed out back for a day or two, until we could get a pen built in the backyard of the house on Broad Street. I guess we were to eventually have our own milk supply, but all I could think about was how beautiful the little creature was. She was black except for a dramatic touch of white on her forehead that reminded me of a star. I named her Venus, for the North Star. The previous owner delivered her, and, to the accompaniment of incessant barking by my dog, Scooter, at the strange intruder, I brushed her until she glowed. After a couple of nervous minutes she liked the attention, and I saw that Venus and I would be fast friends. We put her in the shed, and the next morning I couldn't wait to see my calf. I rushed out to the shed, opened the door—and Venus was lying on the ground, dead. It seemed that Daddy had forgotten about a bag of arsenic he had bought for use as an insecticide, and the calf had chewed through the sack and eaten the contents. My career as a cattleman lasted less than twenty-four hours.

Daddy bought a goat. He either tired of caring for it or intended all along that it be the entrée at a barbecue, for in no time he had it slaughtered.

Again, a black man killed it and barbecued it for a share, and Daddy treated his family and friends to the rest. I looked the other way when the fellow cut the bewildered goat's throat with a butcher's knife.

The man was preparing to haul off the refuse when I asked him for the hide. He was reluctant, but I assured him Daddy wouldn't mind. I had a plan. I spread the thing out on the roof of the shed, raw side up, and tacked it down. I thought it would simply dry out and I would rub it back and forth over a board to break the stiffness and I'd have a tanned hide, just like the pioneers used to do. Well, that must not have been exactly how they used to do. What I got was a rotting skin that was infected with maggots. Gagging all the way, I dragged the thing into the woods behind the house and left it.

I've fancied barbecued goat ever since I lived in Statham, but I never see it anymore. I guess people's tastes are more refined now than they were then. (Try finding real sorghum syrup in a supermarket nowadays.) There was a barbecue restaurant on Highway 29 between Statham and Winder, and for years I'd stop and have a goat sandwich when I was making the trip from Alabama, but it closed, and finally it was torn down, and I haven't eaten barbecued goat since.

I BECAME A teenager in that house on Broad Street. Maybe that helped ensure my love of the place. (Because it's a historic site, I mean.) On August 31, 1949, three months after we moved in, I turned thirteen. Now, we all know a thirteen-year-old has more in common with a twelve-year-old than with a nineteen-year-old, but I was officially a teenager, and no one could turn back the clock. The women in the family had always said, "Bunny's eyelashes are so long and pretty. They should be on a girl." Whereupon I would get the scissors and amputate my eyelashes. Maybe now that I was a teenager they would shut up. After all, I wore campus boots—short brown boots with brass rings attached to the sides—the official emblem of Statham teens.

My newfound status as an elder statesman did not exempt me from cutting the grass and preparing the ground in the backyard for a garden. With a hoe I battled Bermuda grass that resisted with incredibly tangled roots. I spent half the time on my knees, tearing it out of the ground with my hands, cussing it in frustration. The backyard had been a lawn to the family who lived there before, and the Bermuda was entrenched, but Daddy wanted to raise his own veggies, and I was the sharecropper. I decided then and there that I not only would never be a farmer, but that as an adult I would never have a garden, and I never have.

Muscling the push mower over the front yard wasn't so bad. I could tell myself I was getting in shape to play ball, developing my shoulders and arms and legs. Decades later, when we lived in Birmingham, my power mower gave up the ghost. I had romantic memories of the Statham push mower with its whirring blades, drawing an honest sweat and toning my biceps, and I told my wife, Sandra, that since our yard was flat, I was going to buy a push mower. "You'll use it a couple of times," she said. She was wrong. I used it once. Then I did the sensible thing: I bought a power mower and put the push mower in a yard sale. It probably went to another nostalgia-motivated soul who used it one time.

I fashioned a basketball backboard and goal and, with the help of my friends, erected it beside the house on Broad Street. The post was a pair of two-by-fours nailed back to back, and the backboard was of scrap clapboard. We dug a hole and erected the thing and through trial and error eventually got it to the correct depth so that the goal was ten feet from the ground. The entire contraption fell during the process and mashed the goal out of round, but we didn't care. The basketball would go through it and into the net. Goals had always been black, but in 1950 they became orange because a study revealed that color promoted accuracy. Never one to be left behind the times, I bought a small can of paint and painted my goal orange.

I had an old leather basketball with laces, like a football. I had to keep it pumped up to the bursting point to make it bounce on the disturbed ground. The laces wore out and the rubber bladder tried to escape through the resulting slit, but I replaced them with some parachute cord. It never would bounce true after that, but so what?

Wayne Holliday, Jimmy Lowe, Buck Manus, and Chick Bragg didn't think much of my basketball court. It was too easy to get the keys to the school gym from Mr. Barrett, the principal. Mostly I played alone on my court. I didn't mind that the backboard swayed when the wind blew and when the ball struck it. I even invented a professional league and kept up with the standings on a piece of paper that I hid from prying eyes. I was a teenager, but I had not totally put away childish things.

Well, no, I definitely hadn't. I got a goofy-looking Mohawk haircut, and so did Jimmy. I don't remember who else did or didn't. I doubt that Wayne did. He had a nice crop of dark hair, and I have no memory of it being desecrated. Trying to picture Wayne with a Mohawk is like trying to picture Billy Graham with a Mohawk. Jimmy must have said something that scared the barber off. "The barber wouldn't cut it," he remembered in 2007. "Mamma got the scissors and cut it on each side like I wanted it." I had short hair much of the time anyway, so a Mohawk wasn't that much of a stretch. I regret that I don't have a photograph of myself with the Mohawk.

In front of my house was a street light with a corrugated steel shade that was suspended over the middle of the street by a cable. Bullbats dived at the thing, but we saw it as an opportunity to play night football. Footballs used in real games were either white or yellow, so I painted my brown football yellow with some leftover model airplane paint, and we tossed it around under the dim light. That's all we did, toss it around, because even as hardy as we were we didn't care to be tackled on pavement. But that's the kind of things kids did back then, before TV, video games, and air conditioners made them voluntary inmates inside their own homes.

Broad Street was, and is, a street of front porches. Porches are made to sit on. Radios can coexist with porches, but television sets can't, so front porches aren't considered essential in the construction of homes today. Our house had a large front porch with a swing that was suspended from the ceiling by chains and two rocking chairs. Give me a rocking chair, a railing to prop my feet on, a glass of Mother's lemonade, and a copy of *Sport* magazine after a couple of hours of playing ball and I was content.

The last time I was in Statham I sat with Ralph Dunahoo, Emily Colvard, and Ibby Witcher on their Broad Street front porches, and we watched the world go by. When my friend Becky Dunahoo Dunagan wrote a sweet letter of appreciation to her mother, Mayrell Dunahoo, that was published in a newspaper on Mother's Day of 1989, she remembered "rocking on the front porch on warm summer evenings and Sunday afternoons when you knew everyone who passed."

My pals, Beth and Perry Barton, who live in one of the old Broad Street homes, published a fun magazine, *Sweet Tea*, for a while, and Perry's column was titled, logically, "The View from My Porch." In one issue he wrote, "There is nothing quite like a new porch rocker to make a man feel like the king of his castle. To rock, aimlessly, with a glass of ice cold sweet tea, is as close to Utopia as I can imagine."

That sums up the essence of the front porch. Peace, be still. We should build front porches when we build houses. But, then, in this drag-race age, we'd have to force ourselves to use them. It would be the equivalent of getting a push mower. Buying it with all good resolve is one thing; actually using it is another.

Our front porch served as a front row seat for the installation of a sewer on Broad Street, which caused a stir and provided us kids with adventure. They cut one long ditch the length of the street, right down the center. "I remember when they put that sewer system in," Chick Bragg said in 2007. "They had dirt piled up in the middle of Broad Street, and we'd ride our bicycles on top of it." Indeed, if our bikes were not actually involved in an escapade, they provided us the means of getting there. I'd like to know how many miles I put on that bicycle in three years. "They tell me that's why my feet are so flat now, riding that bicycle every day," Chick said.

The sewer project was welcomed, but it wore thin. It seemed to take forever, and it created a muddy mess. Cars that traveled on Broad Street were perpetually in need of washing. It created a soap opera of sorts, too. Some of the workers had their eyes out for the Statham girls. One young woman became enamored of a worker who was quite handsome under all the mud. I remember Daddy saying, "I hope she won't let that situation go too far. When he gets through here he'll leave for another town and forget all about her."

IT WAS WHILE living in that house that I learned to drive. We had a 1940 Oldsmobile that was better than most of the family cars we would own over the years. It was green, and it had an automatic transmission when the vast majority of automobiles were equipped with three-speed manuals. In fact, Hydra-Matic Drive, the first truly automatic gearbox, was introduced in the 1940 Olds. There was no clutch! But the public was cautious about automatics and their diminished fuel economy; their development was stalled when the war prevented manufacture of American cars in 1943, 1944, and 1945, and automatics didn't enjoy widespread popularity until later in the 1950s.

Word of our automatic transmission got around. The town's hot rodders burned rubber with their Ford coupes, sniggering at Daddy and me and saying they wouldn't trade the self-determination of a straight shift for the sissified convenience of an automatic. It didn't faze Daddy, who just laughed with them and told Mother the cops would scrape them off a tree in a curve one day. But I wanted to burn rubber, too. I wasn't interested in being a pioneer.

How big an impression did that car make? I was chatting with Chick Bragg in 2007 when he volunteered, "It's odd what people remember. I remember y'all were about the first people I knew that had a car with an automatic transmission." (For awhile, either in Georgia or Alabama or both, a person who took his or her test for a driver's license in a car with an automatic transmission was limited by law to driving cars with automatics.)

There was a car culture in the South at the time. World War II was over, and soldiers and sailors and Marines had been discharged, and they returned to their towns and farms and bought automobiles. Many had been away from home for the first time, and even if they hadn't seen active duty they were imbued with a sense of adventure. They wanted fast cars with doo-dads hanging off the rear-view mirror and a knob on the steering wheel and rumbling straight exhausts and maybe even a spotlight that could be aimed by the driver.

The car of legend was the pre-war Ford coupe, the Cadillac-powered rocket that whiskey trippers had driven as they hauled 120 gallons of moonshine from Dahlonega to Atlanta and other thirsty destinations—and then raced on Sunday afternoons on dirt tracks, laying the foundation for NASCAR. Returning World War II veterans and other hotshoes didn't have to have a ride that would outrun revenuers, but they didn't want Oldsmobiles with automatic transmissions.

Now, I was just fourteen, but Daddy let me solo in our Oldsmobile. Broad Street was as straight as a pine, and there was no traffic to speak of, and I'd drive from one end to the other, alone in the car. As adults, he and I were different in many ways. I won't back a car out of the driveway without being insured up to my ears, and I wouldn't consider letting a fourteen-year-old drive by himself. At the time, though, I didn't think it was so unusual. After all, when I was in the sixth grade at Tucker I had a classmate who drove a car to school every day.

Something just popped into my mind. I remember that Daddy always bought five gallons of gasoline, rather than stipulating a dollar amount. Jimmy Bryan, who worked for years with me on the *Birmingham News*, said his daddy always bought five gallons, too. There's a scene in an episode of the *Andy Griffith Show* in which Aunt Bee buys five gallons from Goober. Did the glass containers on top of the old gas pumps have a five-gallon capacity?

I am convinced that Daddy expressed his difference, his distinctiveness, in his choice of automobiles. Everyone else had straight sticks on the stalk (the forward gears being low, second and high and the stalk being the steering column), but he had Hydra-Matic. Everyone else had Fords and Chevrolets, but he had the Oldsmobile, a couple of Nashes, a Kaiser (which was manufactured without a hood ornament), an American Motors something-or-other and a Dodge that was so old and decrepit that when he took it to a car lot in Atlanta to make a trade the owner laughed and asked Daddy how much he would pay him to take it off his hands.

My favorite—in retrospect, certainly not at the time—was a Kaiser that I drove daily to Jacksonville State University in Alabama when I was a freshman. The gears were always locking up, and I kept a pick handle in the car to break them loose. I'd jam the pick handle into the gear mechanism under the hood and pry away. There'd come a popping sound and I knew the gears were free—until the next time I parked on a hill.

We lived in Wellington, eight miles from the JSU campus. That old Kaiser used two quarts of oil in the eight miles to school and two quarts in the return trip. I couldn't afford four quarts of oil a day, so what I did was this:

A friend of my daddy owned a filling station, and I asked him to save the oil he removed from customers' cars during oil changes and give it to me. That was what I put in the Kaiser. I'd add two quarts in the morning before leaving for school, and I'd take two quarts with me, in fruit jars. I'd pour them in before I started home in the afternoon. I was well known on campus—not by name, but as the guy with the car that put out a smoke-screen. Of course, the motor blew up one day with all the sound and fury of a motor blowing at Talladega Superspeedway, and that was the end of the Kaiser.

I said it was my favorite car of all those Daddy owned. Only because it affords me that story to tell when I make speeches. I always add that my reusing that worn-out motor oil in 1954 may have made me the first recycler.

If I had been psychic and could have seen that Kaiser in my future I would have been more appreciative of the green Oldsmobile and its Hydra-Matic Drive. After all, I did take Harriette Robertson to ride from one end of Broad Street to the other without adding oil, and the only curiosity for onlookers wasn't a smokescreen but my Mohawk haircut.

Chapter 8

"Let's go to Fesser's and get the keys to the court and shoot some."

Translated, that means: "Let's go to the home of Paul T. Barrett, the principal/coach of Statham High School, and get the keys to the gymnasium and play basketball."

But we never called him Coach. I never heard anybody call him Coach. We called him Fesser, a derivative of professor. Or we called him Mr. Barrett. We never spoke of the gymnasium or the gym. We called it the court. Neither was original with our little gang. He had been Fesser, and the gym had been the court, long before us.

If there were an election to name the number one citizen in Statham's history I believe Mr. Barrett would be the runaway winner. He came to Statham from Buford in 1933 to be the principal, coach, and teacher for a salary of eighty-five dollars per month, two tons of coal, and use of an old house near the school. His wife, Weebie, was upset because there was no indoor bathroom in the house, and Mr. Barrett promised her they'd stay in Statham just one year. But he was principal when Statham High died in 1956, and he was still in Statham when he died in 1983.

Mr. Barrett ran successfully for the post of superintendent of Barrow County schools in 1956, after Statham High and Winder High were consolidated into Winder-Barrow High. "I was present when the votes in the Statham precinct were counted," his son, Bill Barrett, recalled, "and he received 426 votes and his opponent received nineteen votes. I thought this was amazing that one could live in a place so long and only have nineteen votes against him." Some of his friends, though, couldn't imagine nineteen people being against Fesser Barrett, and they reckoned some of them just made an error in marking their ballots.

Maybe it was a reflection of something Mr. Barrett used to say: "Statham is a great place because everybody knows everything about you but they love you anyway."

He not only knew basketball, he knew kids. I played on the boys' basketball team and my sweetheart Harriette Robertson played on the girls' team. The teams were returning from a game on a school bus. I had my arm around Harriette and her head was on my shoulder. We were sitting in the seat behind Mr. Barrett. He turned around, and I thought, "Uh-oh, he won't like this." I should have known better. He had been young once upon a time. He smiled a smile that gave us his blessing.

I was playing for the Statham B team in the little gym at Braselton. We were hopelessly behind with perhaps thirty seconds to go, and one of the teams called time out. In the huddle I blurted, "Come on, we can still win this game!" He smiled, but I knew it wasn't a smile of derision. He was sincerely pleased that one of his players thought like that—even it if it was wildly illogical.

BASKETBALL RULED AT Statham High School. It frequently packed the gym with seven hundred souls, more than the population of the town. In a time when so many teams played deliberate basketball and the two-hand set shot was in vogue, Statham's teams were fast-breakers. "Mr. Barrett was a great guy and a good coach," Fred Ferguson, one of his stars, remembered. "He'd run you to death. You had better be in shape. We ran all the time. We ran, ran, ran. That was our team."

The Wildcats kept the scorekeeper busy flipping the metal numbers on the manual scoreboard atop the boys' dressing room. Statham's 1949–50 team opened the Ninth District boys tournament with a 117–14 victory over Benton. Statham led 51–7 at halftime, and subs played the entire second half. John Mobley Jr., a seventeen-year-old stringer for the *Atlanta Constitution*, phoned in the results from Mr. Barrett's office—but the fellow who answered the phone at the paper didn't believe him.

Mobley was finally able to file his story with a reporter who knew him. He was thankful the next night when Statham defeated Maysville by a score of just 93–10.

Not be outdone by the 1949–50 squad, the 1950–51 Wildcats destroyed Watkinsville 100–34.

Sometimes, when the years have piled up, you think you remember something but it turns out it didn't really happen. Did I really remember that Statham's 1950–51 squad defeated the University of Georgia freshman team? Bill Barrett sent me some newspaper clippings, and there it was:

> Statham High School's unbeaten cagers won their ninth consecutive victory of the early basketball season Tuesday night, defeating the University of Georgia freshmen in a thriller, 38 to 37, in the Statham gym. It was the first appearance of the year for the Bulldog yearlings.

It was homecoming for one of the 'Dogs. "I played basketball and baseball for the Georgia freshmen before I flunked out," Bill Crowe, who had been a member of Statham High's superb 1949–50 basketball squad, told me. "I had mixed emotions about that game. We were playing in the gym where I had played all my life. But it was a big letdown when Statham beat us."

I was in the eighth grade and young enough to be awed by that 1949–50 club, Mr. Barrett's masterpiece, and its all-senior starting lineup. Bill Barrett, Robert Peppers, Johnny Lyle, Jimmy Perkins, and Bill Crowe formed a perpetual motion machine. "We were fast to be white boys," Crowe remembered. "We were fast-breaking all the time. We were all average players. We didn't have a star. The top person probably averaged thirteen points a game and the last person ten points a game. I think we averaged about sixty-six points as a team, and that was a lot in 1950."

"Our record was 37–3, counting the state tournament," Bill Barrett recalled. "We didn't have football, so we started playing in October. We lost two games early, but we had won twenty-five in a row before we lost to Montezuma in the state semifinals."

In the Ninth District tournament those 1949–50 Wildcats defeated Benton 117–14, Maysville 93–10, Banks County 66–22, Braselton 34–32, and Duluth 48–24 to earn a spot in the state tournament at Macon, where they beat Meriweather County 47–40 and Evans 43–42 before losing to Montezuma 37–36.

"Montezuma beat us and then played the next game and won the state championship," Crowe recalled. "The games were in Macon's old city auditorium. It had fan-shaped backboards, and we had never played on fan-shaped backboards. There was an open area behind the goal, and we were used to the wall being right behind the goal. We had trouble adjusting. There were some stands behind the goal, and I bet it was thirty yards to those stands. We'd fast break and end up under the goal, and we couldn't shoot from under the goal. We were pretty much equal with Montezuma, and I'm sure they had trouble adjusting, too. We had never played in a place that big."

Bill Barrett remembered the heartbreaking ending of the semifinal game. Montezuma was freezing the ball, but Johnny Lyle stole it and drove for an apparent game-winning layup with one or two seconds to play, "but an official back at mid-court said he stepped on the line when he stole the ball."

Macon's auditorium, of course, was used for various events besides basketball, so it had to be roomy. At the other end of the spectrum was the gym at Braselton High, one of Statham's regular rivals. I recall that at least one, and probably both, of the back lines in the Braselton gym was touching the base of the wall. You'd better believe that discouraged driving for layups, or "snowbirds," as they were called then. I remember that the local rule was that a player had to be standing on one foot and have the sole of the other shoe against the wall to put the ball in play.

Statham High was in Class C, the lowest classification in Georgia, and no starter on that 1949–50 team was six feet tall. But, to paraphrase, it's not the size of the Wildcat in the fight, it's the size of the fight in the Wildcat.

"Winder was a Class B school, but we didn't have any trouble with Winder," Crowe said. "They had a few big football players, but we always beat them. They tried to slow us down one time when we went to Winder. It was a rainy day, and they waxed the court and opened the doors and let the moisture in on the floor. We took off our shoes and played barefooted and still beat the devil out of them." Since Statham's 1950 population was 626 and Winder's was 4,604, whipping the Bulldogs was mighty sweet.

"Athens High was a Class A school, and Mr. Barrett tried to get them to play us, but they wouldn't do it," Crowe recalled. "They said they had nothing to gain and everything to lose." Indeed, Athens's population was 28,180. And the next season, 1950–51, the Wildcats defeated Class A Ellijay 74–35. A newspaper story referred to "powerful Statham High, current volcano of North Georgia Class C basketball."

Statham put to rout the cliché that height was everything in basketball. "Lilburn had a 6'4" center, and that was big for a Class C school them," Crowe said. "Two of us would close in on him every time he got the ball down low. He liked to squat and then try to come back up and shoot. Jimmy Perkins and I would knock the ball out of his hands before he could come up. Bogart had a big team with some tall boys, but we beat them at Bogart."

Winder was eight miles away and a natural rival, but Class C Bogart was a mere four miles away, and the rivalry was even more intense. "We played Bogart in Statham, and they were undefeated with eight or nine wins in a row, and we had already been beaten that season," Bill Barrett said. "The Statham gym was packed. They thought they could beat us, but we won

50–20. After the game their coach said all Statham had to do was throw any five people out there wearing Statham jerseys and Bogart couldn't have beat them."

Some things never change. I covered college football for forty years, and I regularly observed Alabama and Auburn fans complaining even though their team had won. "Some Statham folks used to bet on the games," Bill Barrett remembered. "One time they gave fifteen points, and we beat Bogart fourteen points, and they were upset."

One larger school wouldn't graciously accept being beaten by Class C Statham High. "Cumming was Class B, and in the 1948–49 season we beat them in Statham," Bill Barrett said, "and then we made the mistake of beating them again in Cumming. When we left they were throwing bottles at the bus. The sheriff followed the bus until it got out of their county."

Gayle Mobley remembered the incident. "I was a mascot or cheerleader or something when Bill Barrett and Jimmy Perkins and that bunch played at Cumming," she said. "There was a fight, and they were throwing bricks at the bus. Mr. Barrett told us to get on the bus and get down between the seats. I was scared to death."

Bill Barrett, Johnny Lyle, and Jimmy Perkins—forward, center, and guard of that 1949–50 club—accepted basketball scholarships to Young Harris College. Barrett also played on the tennis team. "They talk now about girls playing sports with men, but at Young Harris my doubles partner on the tennis team was a girl, and nobody thought anything about it." Zell Miller, a future governor of Georgia, was in Barrett's class at Young Harris. They remain friends.

Bill Barrett was an excellent all-around athlete. As I said, he was a senior in 1949–50, and I was an eighth grader, and as far as I was concerned he was Chip Hilton incarnate. He could do anything Clair Bee's fictional star of Valley Falls High could. I, a hesitant plodder, envied his easy fluidity on the basketball court. He was smart, handsome, and never condescending to the younger kids. Bill gave me a pair of his old leather basketball shoes. They were a size and a half too small, but I scrunched up my toes and wore them every day. He attended a 2006 reunion for Statham High students of the 1950s, and even though he was seventy-three years old, he could have passed for sixty.

But his daddy wouldn't put him at the top of his list of superb Statham athletes.

"He was always honest with me," Bill said. "In 1950 the basketball team I played on had an outstanding year. We won the district tournament and won two games in the state tournament before losing by one point in the semifinals. That same year I went to the state track meet in Macon and won second place in the high hurdles and first place in the low hurdles. I also played baseball, so I was beginning to think I was a pretty good athlete. As you know, the older we got the better we were. I asked Dad the question, 'Who is the best athlete you ever coached?' Without hesitating he said, 'John R. Pentecost.' Reluctantly, I asked him which was the best basketball team at Statham. He said that my team in 1950 was the best—but if John R. had been on our team, nobody would have beaten us."

Statham repeated as Ninth District champion in 1950–51 but lost to Dasher Bible School of Valdosta in the first game of the state tournament. Two teams from the Ninth District went to the state that year. The district runner-up was Braselton—but then Braselton won the state title.

Sonny Morgan, George Lyle, Fred Ferguson, Billy Willoughby, and Sam Wall were the starters. "The most improbable thing was that Statham lost the first seven players off that 1949–50 team, but the 1950–51 team still won the district and went to the state," Bill Barrett said.

I was in the ninth grade and a member of that 1950–51 squad, but I wasn't in the top ten on the roster, so practically all of my playing was on the B team. I didn't even dress out for all the varsity games. I was a typical freshman basketball player, reluctant to shoot, usually passing the ball a split-second too late, easily faked on defense. Either there was a squad limit for teams playing in the state tournament or Mr. Barrett simply decided not to dress out everyone, for he flipped a coin to determine whether Jack Cook or I would be the last man in uniform. Jack won. I thought then, and still do, that justice was done because Jack was the better player. So I accompanied the team to Macon but sat in the stands in street clothes.

WOMEN'S BASKETBALL HAS blossomed, what with Title IX forcing colleges to give females opportunities corresponding to those of men. Voracious cable television must be fed, and women's college and professional hoops is a staple. The incredible success of the University of Tennessee and its coach, Pat Summitt, has helped popularize the sport in the South.

But in the late 1940s and early 1950s the women's game was still hampered by those silly rules that required three forwards and three guards, with no one allowed to cross the center line, so the rules themselves devalued the game. When I moved to Alabama in 1952 I found the high schools didn't even have girls' basketball teams. So even though Statham fielded some strong squads, the interest in girls' basketball didn't compare with the passion for the boys' variety. I do remember that Statham had an overpowering forward named Jean Wilburn who, I think, would have been a star in the modern era with its full-court game that requires all-around skills.

"Mr. Barrett was a good coach," Gayle Mobley told me, "but he wasn't disciplined enough, I don't think, as far as the girls were concerned. Some of the girls would go in the dressing room and smoke at halftime. Harriette Robertson and I didn't smoke, and sometimes we'd just stay outside the dressing room."

Emma Lou Owens, one of our little gang, was a guard, but she didn't want to play forward, didn't resent not shooting, "because I couldn't hardly hit the basket, even in practice."

She did leave her mark, so to speak, on the boys' team. "Some of the girls talked the boys into letting us dye their hair with red cake dye," she recalled. "We did it at Gayle's house, with five guys. We were going to a road game, and they wore caps on the school bus. When they started running up and down the court that red dye started running everywhere. Mr. Barrett really got on the girls, but he didn't do anything to the boys, and they were the ones who let us do it."

(I am reminded of the time my future wife, Sandra, and her friend, Sue Tune, a couple of Alabama school girls, attended a 4-H conference. The pupils were asked to wear something green, since that was 4-H's color. They did. They wore their hair green, dyed by food coloring. They had on white dresses. They got caught in the rain. You can picture the result.)

Joan Smith Hammond, who was one of my classmates, believes hers was the first cheerleading squad Statham ever had. "The cheerleaders had no training, nobody to guide them," she recalled. "Mr. Barrett's niece would come down from Marietta and help us. Statham had no cheerleaders, but she got us started. Bobbie Nell Turner was her name."

Joan can still give a spirited rendition of the cheers of that era:

"Big dog, little dog, floppy-eared pup, come on team and eat 'em up." "Your pep, your pep, you've got it, doggone it don't lose it, your pep." And "Two bits, four bits, six bits, a dollar, all for Statham stand up and holler."

Mr. Barrett began his coaching and teaching career at Cornelia after graduating from the University of Georgia. "He coached the first football team at Cornelia," Bill Barrett said. "He was at Cornelia about eight years and at Buford about three years before he came to Statham. I think he coached everything at Buford.

"When he was coaching football at Cornelia they were playing the Piedmont college freshman team. One Cornelia boy told my daddy at halftime, 'They're running every play over my position.' Dad said, 'I heard the guy who played your position last year telling them to run every play over your position because you're yellow.' After that, the fellow made every play. Dad knew how to motivate that boy."

A DEADLY COMPETITION on foreign soil summoned Mr. Barrett's athletes. "During World War II he was always concerned for the safety of his boys," Bill Barrett said, "Some wrote him letters after they had gone into the service, and others came to see him when they were home on leave. One who visited him in early 1944 was Emmett Hale. In June of 1944 Emmett was killed when he was landing a plane with a bomb that was hung up and would not release. J. T. Harris was killed in a plane crash, and Donald Ross was killed on D-Day. This bothered him greatly, perhaps even more so because my brother, Joe, was on his way to Europe."

Mr. Barrett never got burned out on sports. "After he retired he was given a lifetime pass to any high school athletic event held in Georgia," Bill Barrett said. "He made great use of his pass. When he was eighty years old he went to one of the state high school basketball tournaments in Atlanta at the Georgia Tech arena. He was not allowed to enter the gate that was convenient for him but was told he would have to go to the opposite end of the arena to the pass gate. It was difficult for him to get around, so he protested, but to no avail. Being an avid University of Georgia fan, he said the worst thing he could think of to the gate attendant: 'Yes, and I bet you are for Georgia Tech, too.'"

Mr. Barrett had a marvelous sense of humor. "In the 1930s, when money was in short supply, he went to Atlanta to see an Atlanta Crackers baseball game," Bill Barrett said. "Joe was eight or nine years old and was with Dad, but Dad didn't think he could afford two tickets—they cost twenty-five cents—so he only bought one ticket. He was stopped at the gate and told that the boy must have a ticket. Dad responded that he didn't think the child had to have a ticket. The gate attendant said that only children in arms got in free. So Dad picked up Joe and walked in. The gate attendant was so surprised that he just shook his head and let him go in.

"Another time, while driving in Atlanta, he passed the place where he needed to turn, so he decided to make a U-turn. A policeman yelled at him, telling him he couldn't do that. Dad yelled back, 'I think I can make it,' and drove on."

I have observed that a sense of humor and generosity frequently go together. The combination speaks of one's life view. That's how it was with Mr. Barrett. If at graduation time a student couldn't afford a cap and gown, he made arrangements. If a ball team played out of town and stopped for a hot dog and soft drink on the way home, he saw to it that those who had no money were served along with everyone else.

Bill Barrett recalled the last game he ever attended with his dad. It was the year before he died. "He went to a basketball game in Athens to see Georgia play Alabama. We parked our car on the lower side of the coliseum and I had to hold his hand to keep him steady as he walked up the hill. I remember thinking that this was a reversal of roles because he had held my hand or carried me so many times. When we were inside and watching the game I remarked to him that he was probably the oldest person there that night. He said, 'I bet I have seen more basketball games than anybody here.' I bet he was right."

The gym at Statham school is dear to me and other old codgers who remember when it was home base for outstanding high school basketball teams, and some day it will be dear to the elementary school children who run up and down its floor today. I was pleased when it was named the P. T. Barrett Gymnasium in 2001.

"The gym is certainly considered old as far as buildings go," Bill Barrett said at the dedication ceremony, "but some of you may remember what we used to call the old gym. It was located on the top floor of the old building, which is no longer standing.

"It really was not adequate, so in 1940 the local community determined to build a new gym, even though money was in short supply. At that time the school was under the control of the local school board, not the county. It was a dream of Dad's to have a new gym, and the school board was willing to take on the project of building one.

"Many of the local citizens gave free labor, and some gave of their resources. Most of the lumber used in the building came from trees that were donated by people within the community. A sawmill was set up on the campus on the baseball field about where left field was located. I can remember watching as the trees were cut into lumber that was to be used in constructing the new gym.

"The work on the gym began in 1941 but was slowed by the beginning of the war in December of that year. You will notice that the crossbeams are made of wood instead of steel. The war effort took priority, so steel was not available. Work did continue, and the gym was completed in the summer of 1942.

"The first game was played in the gym in the fall of 1942. My brother, Joe, was a member of the first team to use the gym. I believe that Dad told me one time that the total cost of the gym was $30,000."

I can close my eyes and see Bill Barrett and Gayle Mobley and Fred Ferguson and Jean Wilburn and Jimmy Perkins and Sonny Morgan honoring that court with their basketball skills. Of course, to the rhythm of: "Statham Wildcats on the ball, they've been drinking Hadacol."

Chapter 9

I have a remarkable photograph of the University of Georgia's Zippy Morocco making a long run against Furman in Sanford Stadium in 1950. The remarkable part isn't the long run but that the grandstand in the background was nearly empty.

The game was played on November 25 in eleven-degree weather, and the crowd was estimated at one thousand. Had I not been there the crowd would have been 999.

I was cocooned inside my scratchy wool army-surplus sleeping bag, and the only things that showed were my watery eyes and my Rudolph-like red nose. I huddled against a low concrete wall that extended from the top of the stadium to the bottom and partially blocked the frisky wind. (We knew all about chill wind but not about windchill. I've often wondered what the windchill factor was that day.) Some fans felt sorry for me and shared their hot chocolate, which became lukewarm chocolate as soon as it was poured from its insulated container into a paper cup.

I was fourteen years old. Why was I in such a place on such a day? Because I wanted to see Georgia play football, that's why. It was a great game. Georgia won 40–0. I didn't say it was a close game; I said it was a great game. I would have been there if the temperature had been eleven degrees colder. (Well, I probably wouldn't have been; Mother balked at letting me go as it was, but Daddy said, "Aw, it won't hurt him." But she probably would have won that argument if the temperature had been zero.)

Since Daddy was a railroad station agent, he also was a telegrapher. His depot reverberated with Morse code as he conversed with other railroaders. A Prince Albert tobacco can was inserted behind the receiving instrument to make the drumbeat of the dots and dashes more resounding. I knew about codes and code-breaking from playing World War II, and I thought my daddy must be a very important man to converse in secret sounds.

In those days sportswriters covering football games wrote their stories on portable typewriters and handed the pages to a Western Union representative in the press box. He distributed the stories to telegraphers who dispatched the deathless prose to Western Union receivers for delivery to the newspapers. Occasionally Western Union would ask Daddy to help at Georgia games.

Afterward, as we rode home to Statham in the dark, I would delight in his accounts of sending stories to Pittsburgh, Baton Rouge, Chattanooga, Washington, D.C. Some of the sportswriters he knew by name: "I sent old Sam Glassman's copy to Macon today." He'd repeat some of their leads, and I would smile at the sheer genius of the scribes (as the *Atlanta Journal* called sportswriters).

IF DADDY WASN'T going to Athens on a football Saturday, that didn't mean I wasn't. I'd hitchhike the fourteen miles from Statham and slip into the stadium over the fence behind the east end zone. (I'll admit I probably wouldn't have thumbed to Athens on the day of the eleven-degree Furman game, though.)

My friends and I hitchhiked to Athens frequently. "Georgia has a baseball game with Clemson today," Wayne Holliday might say. "Want to go?" And we'd station our fourteen-year-old selves alongside Highway 29, stick out our thumbs, and in two or three minutes we'd be on our way to Athens. Now, you're probably thinking our parents were negligent. No, they weren't. It was a different United States than the sick one we live in today. Mindless murder and demonic mayhem had not yet rolled wholesale across the landscape. Drugs hadn't begun their theft of the nation's soul. Nobody was surprised to see young boys thumbing. I hitchhiked for years, and never did any Samaritan say or do anything improper.

Now, I was picked up by a drunk once when I was a senior in high school and living in Alabama, but he was a friendly and earnest chap. My pal Donald Arial and I had dug a well, and the money was burning a hole in our pockets, so we thumbed the 120 miles to Chattanooga to see a National Football League exhibition game. (Charley Trippi's Chicago Cardinals were playing!) We were returning in the dead of night somewhere around Fort Payne, Alabama, when a fellow in a 1936 Plymouth rattletrap spotted us and hit the brakes.

We'd have to sit up front with him, he told us. The back seat was full of clothes because he was leaving his wife. He took it upon himself to save us: "Boys, whatever you do, don't never get married." He was drinking straight white lightning and was well into it. I wasn't going to ride with him if he was behind the wheel, so I tactfully pointed out that he could apply both hands to the Mason jar if I drove. He agreed, we turned down his offer to share the moonshine, and off we went, him cussing the shrew he had married and us offering sympathy and assuring him we'd never marry.

ATHENS WAS A magnet to me and other Statham boys. We'd go to swim meets, baseball games, football games, and football practices. We'd thank the benefactor who'd given us a ride and get out at the monument on the main drag (which also was named Broad Street). Usually we'd drop by the poolroom/bowling alley across the way.

The duckpin bowling lanes that extended down one side of the building held no interest for us. The poolroom was another matter. We observed the scornful men who gambled on nine-ball, drawing a bead with their cue sticks through the smoke that curled up from the cigarettes that dangled from their lips. They cursed and furtively slipped the money into the table pockets when they lost so no FBI or CIA or Interpol agent in disguise would spot the evidence lying on the green felt. We wondered if those characters lived in the cue room, as we called it, because they were always there when we were. During the week we might see a Georgia football player sauntering through the poolroom, as cool as could be, his red wool letter jacket with black leather sleeves emblazoned with a black G. We recognized them from their pictures in the newspaper.

Infected by the rebellious atmosphere of the poolroom, we would move purposefully toward Sanford Stadium. I say purposefully because our focus was on breaking into the ballpark and thus avoiding purchasing tickets. We reckoned how many RC Colas, hot dogs, and packs of peanuts we could purchase at Fannie Mae Sims's cafe with the price of admission and thought it folly to hand the money to a ticket taker. We'd just slip in, thank you.

The late Chancellor Steadman V. Sanford's ballpark was a castle to be scaled. Policemen, security guards, and ushers were its defenders. They wouldn't have poured boiling oil on us from the parapets, but they probably would have escorted us out a gate. We'll never know, for we never got caught, not once.

The weakest point was a chain-link fence behind the east end zone. It was buried in honeysuckles and sweet gums and mimosas and blackberry bushes. It's all been cleared since, of course, and now there's a monster grandstand on that end. Even a skinny snake couldn't slip in. After all, Sanford Stadium seats 92,746 today; its capacity back then was 36,000.

We'd hide in the undergrowth and spy out the sentries. When they turned their backs or wandered away we'd scale the fence, battle the strands of barbed wire across the top, and drop to the ground. We were in the stadium but we weren't home free. We were merely behind the dressing room and scoreboard. We peeped around the corner, again scouted out the enemies, and when all was clear we blended in with the paying customers who paraded on the walkway that encircled the playing field.

Jimmy Lowe, Wayne Holliday, and, I think, Buck Manus joined me on these missions. "I don't remember being scared," Jimmy said as we chatted in 2007. "I do remember that I knew I was doing something I wasn't supposed to be doing." Chick Bragg thumbed to Athens with us for some events, but he wouldn't slip into the stadium. "I was afraid my daddy would kick my butt," he admitted in 2007. "You know, he was the policeman for a little while."

Buddy Rutledge was a freshman football player at Georgia who was stricken with polio. They had a benefit game for him that matched the Georgia freshmen and a visiting team. I slipped into the stadium and saw the game for free. Buddy and I roomed together on Miami Beach when Auburn's fine 1963 team met Nebraska in the Orange Bowl. I was then a sportswriter with the *Birmingham News* and he was the Auburn radio broadcaster. I handed him a dollar and said, "I've been owing you this for years." After I explained, Buddy laughed and tried to give the dollar back to me, but I wouldn't take it. "I'm just glad you're not charging me interest," I said.

I ENJOYED ATTENDING football practice on Ag Hill. You just walked up and watched. There was no security, no passes. The Georgia coaches tore into the players as if they were enemies, not men on a common mission. I still remember one assistant cursing quarterback Zeke Bratkowski as if he were a borrowed mule. I wondered why the tall, muscular Bratkowski didn't just punch him in the nose.

Wallace Butts was Georgia's head coach. He was a short, cherubic fellow who was known as the Little Round Man. His appearance belied his aggressive manner of coaching. "You have to pay the price," was the phrase most associated with Butts's methods, and the price was high. Weeping Wally screamed at the players just as his assistants did. Years later, Bill Hartman, one of Butts's aides, and I became friends, and he told me, "Butts opened his practices to the public because he wanted to further his image as a tough guy, as a rugged disciplinarian. He knew onlookers would leave practice and tell others about how mean he was and how rough practice was." Well, I did exactly that.

Butts was called Weeping Wally because he always overpraised the opponents and denigrated his own team in the press. He once convinced Scoop Latimer, a Greenville, South Carolina, sports editor, that his 1946 team—which featured Charley Trippi—was too banged up to defeat Furman. Latimer picked Furman in print—and Georgia won 70–7.

If you lived in Statham you were a Georgia fan, and Georgia Tech was the enemy. I never heard any Stathamite declare for Tech and its great coach, Bobby Dodd. If there was a Tech fan within the city limits I didn't know it. Yet, there was room in our hearts for the legend of Clint Castleberry. It would have been unpatriotic otherwise.

Castleberry played but one year for Tech, his freshman season of 1942, but he finished third in balloting for the Heisman Trophy. His running and punt returning led the Yellow Jackets to a 9–1 regular season and a trip to the Cotton Bowl. After the season Castleberry went into the air corps and disappeared over the Mediterranean. Old Techsters still declare he could have become the best back the South ever produced.

We Georgia fans had our own war-football legend. George Poschner was an All-American end on Georgia's 1942 team who was shot in the head while charging a German machine gun nest. He lay in the snow and ice for more than forty-eight hours. Doctors amputated both legs and fingers on his right hand and put plates in his head. They marveled that he survived—but, calling on the lessons of Georgia football, he not only lived, he learned to walk with artificial legs.

The Tech and Georgia freshman teams played a charity game each Thanksgiving Day at Grant Field in Atlanta. Daddy and I always attended. One year we sat in a drenching rainstorm. Georgia played the first half in red jerseys, Tech in blue—though the colors could hardly be discerned after a few minutes in the mud. Just before the second-half kickoff, Georgia came out of the dressing room in dry white jerseys. I thought that was so clever. Then Tech came out in dry white jerseys, and I was miffed at the imitators. Both teams played the final two periods in white jerseys.

I was awed by anything that had a connection to Georgia football. Butts owned a restaurant named The Huddle in downtown Athens. It was below ground level, and stairs led from the sidewalk. We couldn't afford to eat there, but my pals and I would bound down the steps, saunter inside, soak up the atmosphere for a couple of minutes, and then leave when someone asked, "Can I help you?" We hoped to see Weeping Wally himself, but we never did.

UNDERLYING OUR PASSION for Georgia football was a certain emptiness, though. The male members of our little gang could kid ourselves that we would play baseball for the Atlanta Crackers some day, but we knew we would never play football for Georgia. Kids in bigger towns could dream that dream, but not us, for Statham High School didn't have a football team. The village was just too small.

Teachers and pupils used to reckon that Bill Barrett at quarterback, Johnny Lyle at fullback, and Jimmy Perkins and Bill Crowe at halfbacks would be a marvelous backfield. It was said so much that it became a provincial cliché. But no one really knew. They were fine basketball players for the Statham Wildcats, but they would never have an opportunity to play football.

Football was the one glorious ingredient that was missing from my years at Statham. I was fortunate enough to play football later at Alexandria High School in Alabama (the final stop on my odyssey through the public school systems of three states), and I wouldn't take a million dollars for the opportunity—and I mean that literally—but no one would ever strap on a Statham Wildcats football helmet.

There was periodic speculation that Statham might field a football team "some day." Maybe the enrollment would increase to that point. Maybe Statham could play six-man football, as Tucker High had. Maybe some rich benefactor would foot the bill. Maybe, maybe, maybe. But they closed Statham High in 1956, and that ended the maybes.

BUTTS's 1946 GEORGIA team, captained by Charley Trippi, had gone 11-0, murdered Tech 35-7, and won at least one version of the mythical national championship, but I was just ten years old and had but a passing interest. Two years later, though, I was rabid, and the 1948 squad is still my favorite Georgia club. I kept a game-by-game scrapbook, eagerly whacking away at the Sunday paper with Mother's sewing scissors on Monday.

Those Bulldogs beat every regular-season opponent but North Carolina—which got a ninety-yard punt return from Choo Choo Justice—and they marched off to play Texas in the Orange Bowl. Texas's record was 6-3-1, and Florida writers howled that the Orange Bowl had imported a third-rate team to face Georgia.

That was fine with my pals and me. To us, it sounded like a sure victory for the Bulldogs, despite Weeping Wally's protestations that the Florida writers were providing motivation for the Longhorns. We ate our lunch of hog jowl, blackeyed peas, turnip greens, and cornbread for luck and riches and turned on the radio and prepared to start the new year in the best way possible, celebrating an impressive Georgia victory. But Texas whipped the Bulldogs 41–28, and we were crestfallen.

Three of those 1948 Bulldogs—Gene Lorendo, Buck Bradberry, and Joe Connally—became assistant coaches at Auburn, and, thanks to my job as a sportswriter with the *Birmingham News*, I developed a friendship with them. As a boy in Statham, I couldn't have dreamed of that happening.

Lorendo, especially, was a delight. He was from Minnesota, and after he retired he returned to Minnesota. I kidded him that he was the only person I ever knew who retired and moved north.

He was a huge man with a huge voice and a huge appetite for emotional, kamikaze football. He never lost his Yankee brogue, and its edges weren't smoothed by elements of a Southern drawl. His cusswords would melt an anvil. One time I was in Jackson, Mississippi, to cover a night game involving Alabama. Auburn was playing in the afternoon, and I was watching the Tigers on TV. There in my motel room I could hear the booming, profane voice of Gene Lorendo from the Auburn sideline hundreds of miles away, imploring his players to obliterate the enemy. Those producers have a problem for the rest of this game, I thought.

Lorendo was rough as a cob, but his players loved him. Terry Henley, the tailback of the 1972 Amazin's, remembers Lorendo forcing him to run the same play a dozen or so times in a row in a scrimmage—with the defense knowing what was coming—until he got it right. But you'd better not say a critical word about Gene Lorendo in Henley's presence, even today. Lorendo was a member of Coach Shug Jordan's original Auburn staff that lifted the Tigers back to football prominence after dark years, and he became the most famous assistant coach in Auburn's history.

Lorendo not only played football at Georgia, he played basketball when Jordan was the Bulldogs' head basketball coach. Lorendo told me he and the star of Jordan's hoops squad got in a fight in practice, and the other fellow vamoosed, never to return to the squad. "The best player on the team," Jordan railed at Lorendo, "and the worst player on the team runs him off. Damn."

Big Gene told me he played two years of junior college football and basketball and a year of professional basketball before enrolling in Georgia as a freshman. He said they purposely dropped his file behind a filing cabinet so they could plead ignorance if the NCAA ever checked his eligibility.

Johnny Rauch, the All-America quarterback, was the marquee player of those 1948 Georgia Bulldogs, but I was drawn to a lineman named Porter Payne. The name bespoke a no-nonsense player, and when his posed photograph appeared in the newspaper I noticed that he was smirking, as if he knew he was about to rip the head off some Yellow Jacket or Tiger or Gator.

IN 1981 I wrote a book about Georgia football, *Silver Britches*. Each chapter was about a former Georgia player and what it was like to be on the team during his particular time and about his life after leaving school. I chose Porter Payne to represent his era.

Payne was a prosperous real estate man in the Atlanta suburb of Dunwoody when I interviewed him. He told me about a side of Butts I never could have guessed from watching Wally raging on the practice field when I was a kid. Porter and Mary Payne were married when they were sixteen years old, between their junior and senior years in high school, so he brought a wife with him to Athens. Their first child, Patti, was born before he ever played a game for Georgia. "Guess where we went from the hospital?" Payne asked me. "Coach Butts picked us up, and we went back to his house and stayed three days and three nights. He was getting up in the middle of the night and feeding and changing that baby. He wouldn't wake me because we were practicing football."

The loss to Texas in the Orange Bowl was an omen. Butts had lost his touch. Georgia skidded to 4–6–1 in 1949, and our little gang languished with the Bulldogs as they slipped into mediocrity. Georgia Tech beat them eight straight times (1949–56). Butts had one last hurrah, his 1959 team going 10–1, winning the Southeastern Conference championship and shutting out Missouri in the Orange Bowl. Our little gang by then was beset with the problems of adulthood, but I suspect we said, "Way to go, Little Round Man," each in his own way.

Chapter 10

My mother had just come from the operating room where the doctor's optimism that the cancer was confined to a kidney had been refuted by the evidence before his eyes. The cancer had spread, and there was no hope.

It fell my lot to tell her the bad news that morning in 1989. She didn't panic, didn't cry. She simply said, "Well, I've had a good life. If that's the way it is, that's the way it is."

She mentioned my daddy, Clyde Bolton Sr., who had suffered long and horribly without complaint before dying from emphysema in 1972, and she said she hoped she could be as brave. "He showed us how to live, and then he showed us how to die," she said. What an epitaph, especially coming from the person who knew him best. She got her wish. She had shown us how to live, and then she, too, showed us how to die.

We cared for her at our home in Trussville, Alabama, during the final days, and one of the hospice nurses told us, "Someone will come for her. Tell her it's all right to go."

Sandra went to the store to get her some ice cream, and when she returned Mother said, "Clyde came while you were gone. I wish he could have stayed."

"Did you want to go with him?" Sandra asked.

Mother smiled and said, "Yes."

"Well, it's all right if you go."

Those were the last words Mother spoke. She died the next day, three days after Mother's Day.

I don't believe she was dreaming or hallucinating. She said Daddy came to her, and I believe he did. At his funeral I had asked the minister to read from Ecclesiastes: "To every thing there is a season and a time to every purpose under the heaven: A time to be born and a time to die . . ." I believed that, and I knew it was time for Mother to join Daddy.

Clyde Burnell Bolton and Annice Geneva Storey were married at 6 P.M. on October 12, 1925, at the North Side Baptist Church in Calhoun Falls, South Carolina. He was twenty-one years old and she was twenty. They had two children, my sister Elizabeth Anne—Betty—and me. I'm Clyde Burnell Bolton Jr., though I've never used the junior or my middle name except on official documents. Betty was ten years older than me. "You weren't planned," Mother confirmed my suspicion when I asked, "but you've always been loved, and I'm so glad we had you."

In her bride's book, on the page headed Our First Meeting, she wrote: "As the custom was in the twenties, all churches gave suppers to make money for the church. It was at such an event that we met. I was acting as a waitress as the girls of the church usually did. I had to wait on the table where Clyde sat and his good friend J. W. Sanders introduced us."

What if Clyde hadn't gone to that church social? What if J. W. Sanders hadn't gone? What if someone else had waited on their table? Our lives, our very existences, are blown into being by the most random of winds. What happened on that night so long ago even affects you, because if all those pieces hadn't fallen together you wouldn't be reading this book.

Opposites do attract, at least in the case of Mr. Bolton and Miss Storey.

DADDY GREW UP in Elberton, Georgia, and Statham. His father before him was a railroad man, a station agent for the Seaboard. Mother grew up in Calhoun Falls where her father was superintendent of a cotton mill, a big man in town. Daddy was an extroverted teller of dirty jokes, a creator of turtle stews for his family and neighbors, a fellow who loved fishing and football and stock car racing and a drink of whiskey—including white lightning in that time of widespread dryness in the South—who made friends instantly. Mother was reserved, mannered, a girl who almost married a Baptist preacher before Daddy swept her off her feet.

Over the years she would shake her head incredulously when she told the story of a disastrous act of courtship by her future husband. She and her parents were sitting on the front porch on a Sunday afternoon when her approaching suitor decided they would be impressed if he spun his automobile in the driveway. Alas, he lost control and the car skidded into the front yard and decapitated an upright water spigot, creating an instant surging fountain. They weren't impressed. "Fix it, Clyde," said her father, a man who never got rattled about anything.

I was a little boy when Daddy took me to the first stock car race I ever saw. It was in rural Georgia (near Jefferson, I think) and we watched hot rods churning up the dust on a Sunday afternoon. What I remember vividly is that the spectators sat on a grassy hillside, and a woman sitting behind us had her dress pulled up over her knees and wore no panties. My daddy glanced over his shoulder several times. She grinned and so did he. I thought about how embarrassed she would be if she realized we could see up her dress. Ah, the innocence of youth.

Daddy was a gentle man. I got only one spanking in my life, and it was administered by Mother, who had warned me to stop picking on a younger female cousin. Daddy was unfailingly polite—the word chivalrous comes to mind—to women. He was a soft touch for down-on-their-luck acquaintances who hit him up for loans, though he knew they mightn't pay him back, and he certainly didn't have the money to spare. He was a fun fellow with a long roster of friends, but another side of him emerged in Ponce de Leon Park in Atlanta one night. I was startled when I heard about it. I don't remember who told me the story. I'm sure it wasn't Daddy or Mother. Maybe it was an uncle or one of his friends who accompanied him to the baseball game.

Daddy was sitting beside a young married couple who were in their teens or early twenties, and in front of them were a couple of punks. One reached behind him and rubbed the girl's leg. "Hey, don't do that," her husband said in a shaky voice.

Again he ran his hand part way up her dress.

"Don't do that," the boy pleaded.

He did it again. Whereupon Daddy picked up a beer bottle, broke it over the back of a seat and said, "He asked you not to do that." The two scumbags got up and moved to another section of the ballpark. It was right out of a saloon scene in a Western movie.

Daddy might have been a big old teddy bear, but he was not to be trifled with. One day he was standing outside the depot when he saw an older boy, a repugnant bully, throwing rocks at Wayne Holliday as Wayne rode by on his bicycle. "Stop that," Daddy yelled at him.

"I'll get your boy then," the jerk said. I gulped.

Daddy walked out into the street until they were separated by a couple of feet and said, "You lay a hand on my boy and I'll stomp your ass." I never had a problem with the bully after that.

Daddy believed right was right and wrong was wrong. A man wanted to join the Statham Masonic lodge, but he was blackballed by one member. Daddy thought the blackballing was based on something personal and without merit, and he dropped out of the lodge in protest.

When fire destroyed an antebellum mansion, he said, "I always like to see those things burn because I know what built them." He was, of course, referring to slave labor.

Mother was a housewife, a typical woman of the 1940s and 1950s. She took care of her husband, their kids, and the household. Her specialty was fried half-moon pies, peach and apple, and frequently I'd come home from school to find a hot pie and a glass of cold milk waiting for me.

She also had to take care of her own mother who lived in Williamston, South Carolina, and who was chronically ill. I hated for her to leave because the house seemed empty when only Daddy and I were there. I missed her. I was a mamma's boy, and I don't mean that in the derisive way it's usually intended. I wasn't a sissy. I simply enjoyed Mother's company and she enjoyed mine. We did things together. I could tell her my problems, and she would listen.

If it was summertime I could go to Williamston with her and play with my cousin, Jackie Wilson. We played baseball, football, and roamed the woods. He was an only child, and I think we were the brothers neither of us ever had. Sometimes my other cousins, Dickie and Sandra Ammons, would be there. We'd all sleep on pallets on the floor of Jackie's living room. The first drink of whiskey I ever had was at Jackie's house, when I was in elementary school. We found a bottle in the clothes hamper, poured a capful each, downed it, and pretended to be tipsy.

My memories of my maternal grandparents are sketchy. "Miss Sally" Storey, my grandmother, died when I was nine. I remember her only as a sick woman who couldn't share activities with me. W. T. Storey, my granddaddy, used to take the other cousins and me on Sunday "hikes" through the fields and woods. He let me try to milk his cow, but I wasn't much good at it. Once he told Jackie and me that we could have anything in his country store that cost a nickel. Without his knowledge we each got a plug of chewing tobacco—and, of course, got sick as dogs.

The downside of going to Williamston was that Mother and I rode the train. We could ride free because Daddy worked for the Seaboard, and we took advantage of it, choosing the train for any but the shortest trips. I always got motion sickness—train sick I called it. Not only was there the constant rocking of the train as we went around curves, there was the stink of burning coal if it was pulled by a steam engine or diesel fuel if it was a streamliner.

I still remember the feeling of relief when I stepped off the train onto the metal stool the conductor provided and then onto the ground. I swore that as an adult I would never ride a train again, and except for one thirty-mile excursion with the kindergarten class my wife taught, I haven't.

When I was in high school Daddy rigged up a telegraph key with batteries so I could master the Morse code and someday work for the railroad, but I didn't learn it. I had no intention of following a line of work that would require my children—or me—to move constantly.

MOTHER READ GOOD books, and although I read my share of kid stuff, such as the Chip Hilton sports series by basketball coach/author Clair Bee, I also read her books. I remember being tremendously moved by Lloyd C. Douglas's biblical novel, *The Robe*, when I was in the eighth grade. My appreciation of good writing began at home. I dropped out of college as a freshman, and I never had a writing class or a journalism class, but I spent forty-six years in the newspaper business as a reporter, columnist, and editor and I have written eighteen books. I know writing. Maybe I picked it up at home through some sort of osmosis.

Like so many Georgians of the time, Mother was captivated by *Gone With the Wind*, the book and the film. She was in the crowd at the Loew's Grand Theatre in Atlanta on the night of December 15, 1939, when the movie premiered. No, she wasn't among the prominent 2,031 inside the theater; she was among the estimated 100,000 outside, hoping for a glimpse of Clark Gable, Vivien Leigh, and the other members of the cast. Again like so many Georgians, she was devastated when Margaret Mitchell, the author of one of America's most celebrated novels, was fatally injured when a car struck her as she crossed Peachtree Street in 1949.

Mother enjoyed working in the Statham Baptist Church and our other churches, but it was on this point that she and Daddy were truly opposites. I never knew him to set foot in a church. I don't know why. She and I went to church and, without nagging, she would invite him to join us, but he never would.

They did have in common a love of "riding around." (Maybe it was a quick fix for the peripatetic pair between moves to other towns.) "Let's go to ride," either might say after Sunday lunch, and off they'd go, frequently with no destination in mind. They might ride twenty miles or 120. Sometimes I'd join them.

One day we were nearly to Macon when we spotted some commotion on a railroad track. A lot of people were standing around, gravely talking. Daddy, being a railroad man, stopped the car, and he and I walked up a hill to the scene. Mother stayed in the car.

A man had been hit by a train. I gasped, and for a moment I felt I might faint. The sight of that mutilated body haunted me for weeks. I had never seen such a horror in my thirteen years. I can still see what was left of him, as plain as I see the desk in front of me. He was a black man, and I assumed it was an accident, but in later years I thought back on that place and time—Georgia in the 1940s—and realized it might not have been.

A favorite Sunday destination was the home of Daddy's parents, Dorsey and Netta Bolton, in nearby Lawrenceville. Sometimes Daddy would stop at a location on Highway 29 near Winder, and a bootlegger would come to the car with a fruit jar of moonshine. Daddy would pay him, and we'd continue on our way to Lawrenceville. He and his parents and his sister, Kathleen Bolton, would have a nip while they played Setback, their favorite card game (Mother would join in the game but not the imbibing). Five points were possible in a hand, and the victors, when they swept, would sing out, "Hi, low, jack, joker, and game."

My grandmother and Aunt Kathleen always cooked the same Sunday lunch: fried chicken, mashed potatoes, green beans, squash, and lemon meringue pie.

Netta was an impeccable housekeeper who vacuumed her five-room domicile every day. Mother said she was a fanatic, but as an adult I came to realize that she just liked a spotless house, and I suspected some of Mother's criticism was rooted in the fact that while our house was orderly it wasn't spic and span.

WE DIDN'T HAVE a television set, but my grandparents did. Mamma (my name for Netta) liked professional wrestling, and so did I. Her sister, Jewel Cooper, visited from Atlanta, and those two old ladies got down on the carpet and tried to see up the legs of the wrestlers' tights.

Mamma believed wrestling was on the level, and I never had the heart to tell her it was fiction. She hated such villains as Gorgeous George, Killer Kowalski, Baron Leone, and the Skeleton and loved such heroes as Lou Thesz, Antonino Rocca, Tarzan White, and Nick Carter. (Never mind that Nick Carter and the Skeleton were one and the same, give or take a skeleton costume and mask. He was good old Nick when the script required a babyface, the Skeleton when a heel was needed.)

Television was more a curiosity than anything else in the late 1940s. It was black-and-white, and the screen was small. Broadcasting was not a twenty-four-hour undertaking as it is today. The picture, which had to be constantly adjusted by knobs on the set, was received via an antenna on the roof. The spark plugs of a passing car could throw the picture into disarray. So could an airplane flying overhead. When there was no programming the two or three channels that were available telecast an image called a test pattern for the purpose of getting the picture tuned. The programming frequently was insipid, with local performers and talent shows as standard fare. Unless wrestling or an Atlanta Crackers baseball game was on, I didn't devote much time to television. Wrestling was a staple on early TV because it was compact and easily covered, but Crackers games were televised infrequently.

It wasn't until 1951 or 1952, after we had moved from Statham, that we got a TV set, but Mother loved her radio soap operas, and she went about her housework listening to such fare as *Our Gal Sunday*, which, the announcer told us, was "the story of an orphan girl named Sunday, from the little mining town of Silver Creek, Colorado, who in young womanhood married England's richest, most handsome lord, Lord Henry Brinthrope. The story asks the question, can this girl from a mining town in the West find happiness as the wife of a wealthy and titled Englishman?" Every time I heard that intro I reckoned that an orphan who couldn't find happiness as a rich guy's wife was nuts.

Ma Perkins was another favorite. The program did its job because even today I never think of the busybody of Rushville Center without thinking of Oxydol, the sponsor. Of all things, Ma operated a lumberyard.

LIKE MOTHER AND Daddy, my grandparents, Dorsey and Netta, also were divided on the subject of church. But while Mother attended and Daddy didn't, in this case it was Dorsey who was a churchgoer and Netta who wasn't. He was faithful and served as a Sunday school superintendent, but she never went. I have his old Bible, with W. D. Bolton in gold on the cover. The cover is worn and torn from much use.

Their daughter, Kathleen, who lived with them, never married. She was in love with a soldier who was killed during World War II, and there was never anyone else for her. She worked at Fort McPherson in Atlanta, and on a visit to her office I saw German prisoners of war, who seemed to be in considerably less than maximum security. "They're happy," she told me. "They're glad they were captured, to get out of the mess Hitler made of Germany."

There are two questions on the paternal side of my family that have never been resolved to my satisfaction. One involves Daddy's quitting school, the other my granddaddy's relatives.

Daddy left school after the eighth grade. He told me he had to quit to help support the family. He had been a starter on the varsity football team at Elberton High, and he regretted that he never got to play any more. In later years when I mentioned that to his sister, Kathleen, she said, irritation in her voice, "That is not true. My daddy made us a good living. Clyde quit school simply because he wanted to, not because he had to."

When you're a kid you don't think to ask questions of your grandparents, but some day you'll want to know about your forebears. Dorsey's mother is buried in the cemetery at Statham, but all I ever heard about his father is that he was working under a house, bumped his head on a beam, and afterward suffered mental problems and died in the state insane asylum in Milledgeville, and there he is buried. I suppose it's possible, but it doesn't have the ring of truth. When I was an adult I asked Kathleen if Dorsey had any brothers and sisters. "I don't know," she said. How can you not know whether your father had any siblings?

Dorsey Bolton was born on November 21, 1878, and he died on October 18, 1954. There was a distinct division between grown-up and kid, and we never talked about anything important. I suppose he loved me, but he never said so. I was eighteen when he died, and the years of stiffness in our relationship precluded any curiosity about his life on my part. Now, as an adult, I reflect on the marvels that punctuated his years, and if I could do it over I'd sit him down and question him until he begged for mercy.

He was a man full-grown when the Wright Brothers flew at Kitty Hawk in 1903. How was it spending so much of your life with no planes in the sky? Did he believe flight was possible? Or had he ever even thought about it? Was he numbed by the assassination of President McKinley in 1901 as I was by the assassination of John Kennedy in 1963? What did he think of Teddy Roosevelt?

The Model T Ford was unveiled in 1908. Later, mass production lowered its price and made it the first automobile the average American could afford. Did he buy one? Radios were first marketed for home use in 1920. Was that exciting? He was nearly fifty years old when movies began to talk in 1927. Did he take my grandmother's arm and tell her they were going to the theater to see *The Jazz Singer*, the first talkie?

Did it matter to him that Robert E. Peary reached the North Pole in 1909 or that the Chicago Black Sox threw the World Series in 1919? It must have shocked him when the *Titanic* hit that iceberg in 1912.

Was he alarmed when the Spanish-American War began in 1898? How about when the U.S. entered World War I in 1917? How did he celebrate when the armistice was signed in 1918? He must have known veterans of the War Between the States. What did they talk about?

I don't suppose he played basketball as a boy, did he, since James Naismith didn't invent the game until 1891, way up in Massachusetts? Did he think football would have a future when Georgia, Alabama, and Auburn fielded their first squads in 1892, or did he even notice?

That was a long time ago, 1878. My granddaddy walked the earth when Jesse James, Billy the Kid, the Dalton Gang, the Younger Brothers, Wyatt Earp, Doc Holliday, and even Jack the Ripper did.

I spend time with my grandkids. I tell them about my life. They're probably tired of hearing it, but they'll hear it some more before I croak.

My family took a great interest in the career of Ezzard Charles, the heavyweight boxing champion of the world, as did many others in Lawrenceville. Bill Witherspoon was my granddaddy's black porter at the Seaboard depot, and he was widely believed to be the father of the champ. I knew Witherspoon well. I hung on his every word as he passed on his railroad lore to a little white boy. One day I left a cafe near my granddaddy's depot with a hamburger, and some black boys threatened to beat me up if I didn't give it to them. Bill Witherspoon came to my rescue and shooed them off.

We were excited in 1949 when Charles scored a fifteen-round decision over Jersey Joe Walcott to win the championship. The title had been left vacant when Joe Louis retired. We were disappointed in 1951 when Walcott knocked out Charles in seven rounds to take away the crown. There was a quirk in Charles's record. In 1947 Sam Baroudi had killed Glen Smith in the ring; in 1948 Charles's punches caused a hemorrhage in Baroudi's brain and Baroudi died.

Franklin Delano Roosevelt was my family's foremost hero. My grandparents and my parents had known the horror of the Great Depression, and they were convinced the thirty-second president rescued the nation. I would have pitied anyone who said to my grandmother's face that Roosevelt's programs were too socialistic. People needed help, not theories. I have a decorative plate bearing Roosevelt's likeness on display in a china cabinet in my home. I inherited it from Aunt Kathleen, who inherited it from my grandparents.

My folks felt an added relationship to Roosevelt because he spent so much time in Georgia, at Warm Springs. He was there when he died on April 12, 1945. He was resting for an upcoming organizational meeting of the United Nations. He was in the living room of his cottage posing for a portrait. Suddenly he touched his forehead and said, "I have a terrific headache," and he lost consciousness. Three hours later he was dead from a cerebral hemorrhage. I was just eight years old, but I remember the overwhelming sadness that enveloped the teachers at Home Park School and all our neighbors and friends in Atlanta.

MY PARENTS HAD a hard time during the Great Depression. Daddy was laid off from the railroad. He and Mother tried to run a cafe without success. He told me about hungry freeloaders drinking ketchup from the bottles on the table and not ordering. He worked for a loan company, but one day he told his boss he just couldn't repossess another piece of furniture from a poor family, and he quit. "Son, don't ever borrow money from a loan company," he told me repeatedly over the years, even into my adulthood.

Daddy was hitchhiking during the Great Depression, and he reached the Georgia town of Danielsville during the night. There is a statue on the town square of Danielsville's favorite son, Crawford W. Long, the first physician to use ether as surgical anesthesia, in 1842. Daddy slept at the base of that statue. Every time we passed through Danielsville he would point to the statue of the man who prevented so much suffering and say, "I spent the night with old Crawford W. one time."

I had good parents who loved me, and for that I am grateful. We always had three square meals, but we had few of the extras that add zest to life. We usually lived in rented houses with nondescript furniture. We always had previously owned (to use today's pretentious term) cars, some of them downright junk. I dressed in clean but cheap clothes and rarely had the sharp shirts, pants, sweaters and shoes that a kid naturally wants. I was the first baseman on the Statham High baseball team, and I dreamed of having a state-of-the art Trapper mitt, but I had to settle for a cheaper, worn-out old style model—until I was sixty years old and ran across a Trapper mitt in an antique store and bought the damn thing for six times what it cost originally.

I don't know why we lived like we did, because a man with the responsibilities of a railroad station agent must have made a decent salary. My paternal granddaddy had a similar job, and they had a considerably higher standard of living than we did.

Daddy smoked constantly, unfiltered Camels (the brand the advertisements said was preferred by more doctors than any other), and he died of emphysema on April 8, 1972. The years of being subjected to thick, black train smoke may have contributed, too.

Everybody smoked back then, or at least it seemed like it. A survey in

1950 estimated that between forty-four and forty-seven percent of Americans eighteen years of age or older smoked at least one pack of cigarettes a day. (Watch old black-and-white movies and observe how much puffing is going on. Even wise Sheriff Andy Taylor smoked occasionally on the *Andy Griffith Show*, years later.)

The public simply wasn't aware of the dangers of smoking. After all, there was ruggedly handsome actor Kirk Douglas in a magazine ad assuring the reader: "Chesterfields are so mild. They leave a clean, fresh taste in my mouth." His golf clubs were at the ready, so smoking must be the stylish thing to do.

Advertising was a major factor in the increasing popularity of smoking. In 1951 Phillip Morris became the first cigarette maker to sponsor a TV show and spent more than three million dollars on the *I Love Lucy* show.

I loved Lucy, too, but I didn't love seeing my daddy with an oxygen tank as a constant companion, gasping for breath and unable to enjoy the activities a man his age should have enjoyed as a matter of course. He had looked forward to retiring at age sixty-five, but he didn't have many good days afterward, and he was dead at sixty-seven. He was living in Birmingham when he died, but he wanted to be buried in the town cemetery in Statham, beside his parents, and he was.

Mother, who didn't smoke, lived seventeen more years without Daddy. She was eighty-four and a resident of Trussville when she died. There is a marker with her name on it in the cemetery in Statham, but she isn't there. She donated her body to the medical school of the University of Alabama at Birmingham for research. I thought it was a nice gesture.

Chapter 11

Try to imagine life without television. I don't mean the agonies of withdrawal you'd suffer if television went away tomorrow, never to return. I mean life if you'd never had television. We didn't have a TV set when I lived in Statham, but I didn't feel deprived, any more than I feel deprived today because I don't own a Ferrari.

The only person in our little gang with a television set was Gayle Mobley. Her parents, Jesse and Polly, had a grocery store, and they saved every half-dollar that came in and bought a TV. I watched the occasional Atlanta Crackers baseball game that was televised, but if I watched anything else at Gayle's I don't remember it.

In 1950, ninety percent of the homes in America had radios, but only ten percent had television sets. I'd bet that far fewer than ten percent of Statham households had sets. I can remember watching TV at only one other home in the town, and I don't remember who lived there or why I was invited. I remember the screen was round.

The first television broadcast occurred in 1927, but essentially the years after World War II were the pioneer years. The Great Depression and the war had restricted research and ownership of sets. The 1950s were the first decade in which TV had a major presence in the United States.

By 1951 more than twenty percent of the homes in America had TV sets, by 1952 more than thirty percent, by 1953 more than forty percent and by 1959 nearly ninety percent. The joke was that folks were going to have TV if they couldn't have anything else, and you could ride through the countryside and see shacks that were held up only by their television antennas.

I remember crowds standing outside the windows of stores in Athens at night, watching the TV sets that were on display, transfixed by the picture even though they heard no sound, laughing at Uncle Miltie though they didn't know what he was saying.

It wasn't until 1951 or 1952, when we lived in Winder, that my folks got a TV set, but what we did have was radio, and the radio programming of that time was more like the TV programming of today than the radio programming of today. Dramas, comedies, soap operas, quiz shows, programs for children—this was what our little gang and their parents and the rest of Statham's burghers listened to. I started to write that it was today's TV without the picture, but there was a picture. It just wasn't on a screen: it was in the listener's mind. You had to use your imagination. It was a plus that fictional characters and scenes could look any way you wanted them to look.

THE RADIO CHARACTERS differed from my real friends in that I didn't move away and leave them. Jack Armstrong and the Green Hornet moved with me. They were my companions when I lived in big old Atlanta, and when I moved to little old Clinton there they were, stepping out of the boxcar along with our radio. I cherished their faithfulness. Statham, Georgia? Sure, they said, we'll be there. Radio's sound effects wizards lubricated your imagination, and if they were doing their jobs expertly you didn't know they existed. Hoofbeats, traffic noise, chirping crickets (to introduce a rural scene), thunder, dogs barking, gunfire, winging birds, closing doors, airplanes, the roar of the ocean—all were commonplace sound effects that made comedy and drama effective.

A woman's footsteps and a man's footsteps would have their distinctive sounds so the listener wouldn't be confused. The speed of the steps would tell the listener whether the person was running from an attacker or sneaking up on a victim. One sound effects man wore tight-fitting shoes with wooden soles and heels and stood on a board and produced everything from two men running to a woman laboriously climbing stairs.

Coconut shells cut in half and pounded in a box of dirt signified the approach of mounted cowboys. A big balloon holding birdshot and shaken vigorously worked for thunder. Some sounds, such as those of traffic and airplanes, were simply recorded and played back.

Sound effects in dramas usually were subtle, but in comedies they frequently were exaggerated. The most famous comedy sound effect was that of the contents cascading out of Fibber McGee's closet each week.

Some specialized. For instance there were baby criers, screamers, and animal imitators. There were women who on cue could bawl, gurgle, and whine like infants. Actresses didn't like to scream because of the danger of straining their voices, and most couldn't scream convincingly, so specialists delivered blood-curdlers. A seventeen-year-old girl, Nancy Kelly, was the designated screamer for *Gangbusters*, *Front Page Farrell*, and the *March of Time*. It was said that a couple of noted animal imitators, Brad Baker and Donald Bain, could imitate anything from a canary to a pride of lions.

People today take FM broadcasts for granted, but the broadcasts we heard during my Statham days were in AM. FM provides a higher quality sound, but it doesn't have the range of AM. Most radios weren't even equipped with FM bands back then.

My favorite program, hands down, was the *Colgate Sports Newsreel* starring Bill Stern. I suspect there are plenty of geezers my age who can still sing the theme song from memory:

> Bill Stern the Colgate shave-cream man is on the air, Bill Stern the Colgate shave-cream man with stories rare. Take his advice and you'll look nice, your face will feel as cool as ice with Colgate Rapid Shaving Cream.

Bill Stern's stories were, indeed, rare—in fact, some were so rare as to be well distanced from the truth. Stern was a famous sportscaster who milked everything for all the drama that could be extracted, no matter how hokey. "Good evening, ladies and gentlemen," he began the opening. "This is Bill Stern bringing you the 250th edition of the Colgate shave-cream *Sports Newsreel*, featuring strange and fantastic stories, some legend, some hearsay, but all so interesting we'd like to pass them along to you!" Maybe using the words "fantastic" and "hearsay" covered his rear end.

Stern was the most famous sportscaster of his day. He covered college bowl games, NFL championship games, major league baseball, the Olympics, and most of Joe Louis's title fights, and his weekly *Sports Newsreel* was one of the most listened-to shows in radio history. He frequently topped off his dramatic stories with: "Portrait of an athlete." That gave me goosebumps.

THE PROGRAM WITH the strongest product identification for me was *Jack Armstrong, the All-American Boy*. Jack could do anything, from scoring touchdowns for Hudson High to solving crimes to thwarting Nazi saboteurs. You could send in coins and Wheaties box tops and receive a Jack Armstrong whistling ring, a Jack Armstrong pedometer, or a Jack Armstrong secret decoder. The accompanying theme song:

> Have you tried Wheaties? They're whole wheat with all of the bran. Won't you try Wheaties? For wheat is the best food of man! They're crispy and crunchy, the whole year through. Jack Armstrong never tires of them, and neither will you. So just buy Wheaties, the best breakfast food in the land.

I can remember commercials from more than a half-century ago, but I can't, as the saying goes, remember what I had for breakfast this morning. I don't think it was Wheaties.

I listened to the *Green Hornet*, a mysterious crime fighter whose airtime was signaled by the stirring music of *Flight of the Bumblebee* by Rimsky-Korsakov. "He hunts the biggest of all game!" the announcer told us. "Public enemies who try to destroy our America!" There was a blast of music, and then the announcer continued: "With his faithful valet, Kato, Britt Reid, daring young publisher, matches wits with the underworld, risking his life that criminals and racketeers, within the law, may feel its weight by the sting of the Green Hornet." (Looking back on it now, I realize what a clumsy piece of writing that was, but when you're sitting on the edge of your chair, waiting for the Hornet to strike a blow for democracy, you don't analyze syntax.)

Britt Reid was publisher of the *Daily Sentinel*, and Kato was his Japanese valet—until after December 7, 1941, when he suddenly became "Reid's faithful Filipino valet." A secret passageway led from Reid's apartment to a supposedly abandoned building which housed Black Beauty, the Hornet's superpowered, streamlined car in which he and Kato zipped all over town, solving crimes. An added twist was that the Hornet was such a mysterious figure that the cops were always trying to capture him. They never did, of course. He temporarily immobilized criminals with a gas gun and vamoosed just before the police arrived, leaving his Green Hornet seal.

The Shadow was another of my favorites, perhaps the strangest of the crime fighters who darted across the screen of my mind. The Shadow was Lamont Cranston, a wealthy young man-about-town who in the Orient had learned "the hypnotic power to cloud men's minds so they cannot see him."

In a strange, chilling voice, the Shadow advised: "The weed of crime bears bitter fruit. Crime does not pay." And we were told in the same tone: "Who knows what evil lurks in the hearts of men? The Shadow knows!" It was followed by a hideous laugh.

The Lone Ranger, Hopalong Cassidy, the Cisco Kid, and Captain

Midnight were other good guys who carried on the fight for decency. The Ranger and Hoppy and Cisco nailed villainous cowboys, but the captain and his Secret Squadron nailed Nazis.

SOME COMEDIES FEATURED teenagers, and they were favorites among our little gang. The Aldrich family was a staple. Henry Aldrich always sounded as if his voice was changing, and we boys could identify with that. *Meet Corliss Archer* and *A Date with Judy* were delights. Corliss and Judy Foster looked exactly like I wanted them to look, but I didn't think they were as cute as Gayle Mobley.

Our Miss Brooks was a popular high school comedy, and it made a successful transition to television. Connie Brooks, played by droll Eve Arden in both mediums, was an English teacher. Mr. Boynton was a bashful biology teacher who frustrated Miss Brooks by never realizing she was coming on to him. Mr. Conklin was the principal, and his daughter Harriet, Walter Denton, and Stretch Snodgrass were students.

Today's television is a cesspool, vulgar to see and hear, but entire families could listen to the radio programs of my Statham days without embarrassment. Mother, Daddy, and I regularly sat together at night while the trusty old Zenith table model brought us the adventures of Frank Merriwell or the misadventures of Lum and Abner.

Daddy liked detective dramas, *Gangbusters, The Fat Man, The Thin Man, The Falcon, Bulldog Drummond,* and *Sam Spade* could unravel any mystery. *Gangbusters* came on to the sound of marching feet, machine gun fire and the wail of sirens—and thus gave birth to the expression "coming on like Gangbusters."

Radio dramas helped create an atmosphere of adventure about newspapering. Some reporter was always solving a murder. I loved those stories, but there's no connection between my becoming a newspaperman and my having tuned in *Front Page Farrell, The Big Story, Big Town,* and *Casey,*

Crime Photographer. I not only never solved a murder during my newspaper career, but when a thug threatened to "get" me because of the story I'd written about his having a cache of dynamite in his house, I called the cops to protect me.

There were some magnificent comedians during the old days of radio. Again, they made you laugh without the filthy language and lewd innuendo of what passes for comedy on television today. Radio comedy was more difficult to achieve than its counterpart on television. Facial expressions, moves and scenes all contribute to the TV comic doing his job, but the radio comedian had only his words and occasional sound effects. He depended on the listener's imagination to draw the picture.

My favorite comedy was *Fibber McGee and Molly*. The stories were secondary to the cast of characters. A scenario was established and then memorable characters entered the home of the McGees at 79 Wistful Vista to advance or impede the action. Throckmorton P. Gildersleeve, Doc Gamble, the Old Timer, Mayor La Trivia, Wallace Wimple, Beulah, Sis, Mrs. Uppington, and Old Lady Wheedledeck were in the corps that kept things hopping for the McGees.

Catchphrases from the show became embedded in the public consciousness. "That's purty good, Johnny, but that ain't the way I heered it," the Old Timer would respond to one of McGee's pronouncements. "Way I heerd it, one feller says to the other feller, saaaaay, he sez . . ." *Fibber McGee and Molly* was on the air on Tuesday nights, and on Wednesday I was likely to be disrupting a conversation with, "That ain't the way I heerd it, Wayne."

A highlight of the show was Fibber's opening his closet door. "Here it comes!" must have been said in thousands of homes as the script set up the closet moment. Always he opened that door to the consternation of Molly, who knew what was going to happen. As soon as the door opened, everything in the closet fell out, pots and pans, bowling balls, golf clubs—

whatever the listener imagined was falling out. The cascade ended with the tinkle of a little bell and McGee saying, "Gotta straighten out that closet one of these days."

Of course, the writers of a modern comedy would have the actor utter profanity, but the closest Fibber ever came to cussing was this trademark line, "Dad-rat the dad-ratted telephone." Or chair, or newspaper, or light bulb, or whatever.

Harlow Wilcox was Fibber's and Molly's announcer, and the gig made him one of the most famous announcers in the land. The show was sponsored by Johnson Wax (which must have benefited handsomely from the partnership), and, to Fibber's consternation, Wilcox guided their conversations into commercials for Johnson's Wax. McGee demonstrated his disapproval by calling the announcer Waxy Wilcox.

Fred Allen and Jack Benny were master radio funnymen whose "feud" spiced up the *Fred Allen Show* and the *Jack Benny Program*. The feud began on December 30, 1936, when Allen criticized Benny's violin playing. Benny picked up on the remark on his next broadcast, and the needling went on for years.

Not only was Allen one of the great comedians in radio history, he was one of the great writers. He wrote ninety percent of his programs. One of his best lines was this definition of Hollywood: "You can take all the sincerity in Hollywood and put it in a flea's navel and have room left over for three caraway seeds and an agent's heart."

A hit was his visit to the houses in Allen's Alley. Among the memorable characters who lived there were Senator Beauregard Claghorn, a blustering Southern politician; Mrs. Nussbaum, a Jewish housewife who frequently got names wrong; Titus Moody, a reticent New Englander; and Ajax Cassidy. a loquacious Irishman.

Running gags on the *Jack Benny Program* were Benny's screechy violin playing, the sound of his Maxwell automobile, his perpetual age of thirty-nine, his stinginess, his blue eyes, the polar bear that lived in his basement, and the superior common sense of his valet, Rochester. A memorable scene had a holdup man telling Benny, "Your money or your life!" The only sound was the studio audience laughing because they knew the miserly Benny was trying to make up his mind. The holdup man finally repeated his demand, and Benny said, "I'm thinking it over!"

Ventriloquist Edgar Bergen, with his dummy, Charlie McCarthy, was a radio phenomenon. Wouldn't a ventriloquist have to be visible for his act to be meaningful? Apparently not, for Bergen and Charlie and his other dummies, Mortimer Snerd and Effie Klinker, were tremendously popular. Charlie always got a laugh by kidding Bergen that his lips were moving.

Some of the scary programs kicked my imagination into overdrive. *Lights Out* usually came on late at night—for a while, at midnight—which heightened the tension. "It is later than you think," the announcer said ominously in measured words. *Inner Sanctum Mysteries* opened with mysterious organ music and a squeaking door and was my favorite in that category.

MOTHER'S SOAP OPERA fare consisted of such tearjerkers as *The Guiding Light, Life Can Be Beautiful, Pepper Young's Family, Young Dr. Malone, The Right to Happiness, Young Widder Brown, The Brighter Day, John's Other Wife*, and the sappiest of all, *Stella Dallas*. I didn't make a habit of listening to them, but I was exposed to them, and elements of each still ring in my mind.

I came across the opening for *Stella Dallas* when I was doing research the other day, and it came back to me as if I'd heard it an hour ago instead of nearly sixty years ago: "We give you now, *Stella Dallas*, a continuation on the air of the true-to-life story of mother love and sacrifice, in which Stella Dallas saw her own beloved daughter Laurel marry into wealth and society, and realizing the differences in their tastes and worlds, went out of Laurel's life." I remember that I considered Laurel a spoiled snot and Stella an idiot for humoring her.

A kid's mind is like a sponge, and I soaked up radio commercials. Just the other day I found myself mouthing the Pepsi-Cola jingle while I raked leaves:

> Pepsi-Cola hits the spot,
> Twelve full ounces, that's a lot.
> Twice as much for a nickel, too.
> Pepsi-Cola is the drink for you.
> Nickel, nickel, nickel, nickel
> Trickle, trickle, trickle, trickle.

You know that's an old commercial because it's been a long time since you could buy a Pepsi-Cola for a nickel. "Twice as much" was aimed at Coca-Cola, the market leader. Indeed, I bought Pepsis, Royal Crown Colas, and Double Colas because there was twice as much. I never bought Cokes.

The Royal Pudding commercial sticks in my mind:

> Royal Pudding.
> Rich, rich, rich with flavor
> Smooth, smooth, smooth as silk.
> More food energy than sweet fresh milk.

I liked Pepsi and pudding, but a commercial for a product I never used is also indelibly on my brain:

> Super Suds, Super Suds,
> Lots more suds with Super Suds.
> Richer, longer lasting, too,
> They're the suds with super-doooo.

Many a summer night I walked along Broad Street and heard the sounds of radios through open windows. There was no air conditioning, and the windows provided cross ventilation. I heard the people laughing at *Amos 'n' Andy*, and I heard the gunfire from *A Man Called X*, and I heard the dramatic intonations of the *Lux Radio Theatre*. I heard Walter Winchell denouncing communists and spreading Broadway gossip.

Winchell was America's most famous newsman, a newspaper columnist whose Sunday night radio broadcast was one of the highest rated programs in the history of the medium. Men, women, and children stopped what they were doing when they heard his urgent staccato opening, accompanied by the dramatic rat-a-tat-tat of a telegraph key: "Good evening, Mr. and Mrs. North and South America and all the ships at sea. Let's go to press!"

It was an arch example of radio's theater of the mind, because when Winchell later attempted TV he came across as old, uneasy, and mechanical. Television, in a word, demystified him. The disappointing ratings proved that he simply didn't transfer to the tube.

He spoke four words that could have been an epitaph for the golden age of radio: "Television has changed everything."

Chapter 12

As a world-class prank, someone once put a cow on top of the jailhouse in Statham.

Or maybe it wasn't the jailhouse. Maybe it was another building. Or maybe it wasn't in Statham. Maybe it was in Athens.

Or maybe it didn't happen at all.

I heard about the cow on the calaboose when I was a boy living in Statham. The deed was said to have occurred in the misty past. Naturally, I didn't give it much thought. I was more concerned with treating my baseball glove with neatsfoot oil and keeping my ragged bike out of the pits. Years later, when I was interviewing some longtime Statham residents as research for my novel, *Water Oaks*, I heard about the cow caper again, and I became interested.

(At this point I should detour to explain that a calaboose is a jail. The word, of Spanish derivation, was commonly used when I was a boy, but it seems to have lost currency. Several young folks who read *Water Oaks* informed me they'd never heard of a calaboose.)

I was told the pranksters led the cow up the steps to the second floor of the Masonic lodge and walked it across a ramp to the top of the jail, and there the startled townspeople found it the next morning.

"No, no, it wasn't the Masonic lodge," someone else said. "They led it up the steps inside the old hotel."

"They put it on one of the store buildings on Jefferson Street," another testified.

"Wasn't in Statham," another told me. "Some college boys led a cow up the stairs in a building at the University of Georgia. That must be what you're thinking about."

"I'm surprised you don't know all about it," another said. "I always heard your granddaddy was one of the fellows who did it."

"Your granddaddy Dorsey?" an ancient townsman mused. "Naw, I never heard of him being involved in anything like that."

I would like to believe that Dorsey Bolton was one of the pranksters, but I don't. It's delightful to imagine him navigating a cow to the top of a jailhouse, but I can't picture my proper granddaddy doing that, even as a youth. I don't know much about his young years, but I know for a fact he was a member of the school board in Statham in 1915, for I saw his name on an old graduation program. He was a Sunday school superintendent in Lawrenceville. He was a trusted agent of the Seaboard railroad in both towns. His daughter, my aunt Kathleen, told me she had never heard such a thing. I believe if he had been involved he couldn't have kept it to himself all these years. Why would he want to? I'd want everyone to know I had been part of such an epic prank.

My cousin Mote Smith, who was in his eighties when he died in 2007, lived in Statham for many years. There was a cow, and it was put on top of a building, probably in the early 1920s, he said, but it wasn't the jail. He believed it occurred on a Halloween night. A man named Green Arnold lived across the railroad tracks, and he spotted some boys trying to maneuver a cow to the top of a building on Railroad Street. Arnold grew impatient and declared they were sadly inept at putting a cow on a rooftop, so he offered to help. When the job was completed he returned home to milk. Whereupon he exclaimed, "Lord God, I helped put my own cow on top of that building!"

"That happened," Mote said firmly.

WATER OAKS IS set in 1950 in a small Georgia town, the fictional Hempstead, which is modeled after Statham. In it, four teenaged boys decide to kidnap a cow from the pasture of a crusty old farmer, Paris Warner, and deposit it atop a building and thus assure themselves of that peculiar small-town immortality that accrues to those who participate in legendary events, such as being killed at a railroad crossing.

In my fictional version, I have them lead the cow up the steps of the Masonic lodge and walk it over a ramp to the flat top of the calaboose. They stand outside and admire their handiwork for a couple of minutes. They figure they've gotten away with it, but they didn't know Ned Bracey, the town drunk, was in the calaboose.

"But the sound of a voice struck them with the force of a sledgehammer," I wrote. "'I thought I'd seen it all,' Ned Bracey said, his grinning teeth showing between the bars in the narrow slit window of the calaboose, 'but I'll be a suck-egg dog if I ever saw anything like that.'"

Ned takes pity on the kids and doesn't rat them out, even after the mayor offers to free him if he'll finger the kidnapers of the cow, which is named Maybelle Warner. But Archie Fant, the town policeman, does some detective work and identifies the guilty parties. He's a kindly sort, and he lets them off the hook. Fant tells the boys that Ned Bracey must have seen the fellows who put the cow on the calaboose, but . . .

> "Funny thing, Ned and me were talking through the bars this morning while Maybelle was walking around on the roof over our heads, just a few minutes before the mayor arrived, and I never even thought to ask him. It's some policeman who wouldn't think to ask the only witness, isn't it? I must be getting old.
>
> "If I caught the ones that did it, the mayor'd have their hides sure. But, you know, I think there's something involved in this stunt that I'd call overriding factors. I think Ned Bracey thinks the same thing.

"I mean, a hundred years from now people in Hempstead will talk about the cow that got put on top of the calaboose. The story'll get twisted around, and some'll say she was on top of the picture show, and some will say it was the cafe, and there'll be a dozen different versions of how she got up on whatever it was she was up on. But there'll still be the story. So I wonder how much of a crime something is that provides a story like that.

"There was a fellow named Emerson who wrote essays a long time ago, and they're full of good sense, and I read 'em a lot at night. Y'all ever heard of him? He said, 'The years teach much which the days never know.' I think that's just full of good sense. I think it applies in this case, too.

"Don't get me wrong, If I had known anybody was going to get that cow, I'd have stopped them. If I'd seen them putting her on top of the calaboose, I'd have prevented it. But since it's done, I don't guess it's necessary to hang anybody.

"I remember when I was a kid, me and my cousin unhitched my uncle's mule and pulled the wagon off and hid it behind a neighbor's barn. My uncle just laughed, but my daddy whupped me good and said when I got grown I'd understand why he did it. But I didn't, and I still don't."

One of Statham's old timers told me another story that I converted for use in *Water Oaks*. He said a prominent resident had whiskey shipped into the dry town by train. A shady character watched as the wooden barrel was placed in the depot freight room, noting exactly where it was. That night he got under the depot with some lard cans, bored a hole through the floor and the bottom of the barrel, and caught the liquor as it flowed. When the owner came to get his whiskey, he and the depot agent found an empty barrel in a room that had been securely locked. In *Water Oaks* the whiskey is a high-proof tonic and Ned Bracey gets caught stealing it, and that's why he is in the calaboose when the cow is kidnapped.

WHEN I LIVED in Statham there was a prominent daily reminder of a sensational 1925 killing. I was especially awed by it because one of my kinfolks was the killer. I hoped to work a fictional account of the incident into a novel but it didn't fit. Maybe someday it will.

A wide strip of tape slashed diagonally across the plate glass window of the Bank of Statham on Railroad Street. A bullet had pierced the window and created a long crack. The window was held together by the tape and a bolt that extended through a block of wood on the outside, the bullet hole, and a block of wood on the inside.

Mrs. Dick Bowman shot and killed Guy Thurmond, a businessman and well-known citizen. She was my grandmother Netta Bolton's first cousin. Some of us kids used to reenact the shooting of Guy Thurmond on the sidewalk in front of the bank, which had been closed since the early 1930s. The broken, taped window might as well have been a historical marker identifying the O.K. Corral.

Thurmond had shot and killed her husband, Dick Bowman, on November 11, 1924. Thurmond said Bowman shot at him first. On May 12, 1925, Mrs. Bowman got her revenge by pumping five bullets into Thurmond.

Carl Hale operated a tax service in the old bank building. I stopped by a few years ago, and he showed me a bullet hole in the ceiling. He was a relative of Guy Thurmond, and I was a relative of Thurmond's killer, but we could joke about it. "I'm not interested in a Hatfield and McCoy feud," I said. "Me, either," he agreed.

THE NODOROC APPEARS in *Water Oaks*, although I moved it from its location between Statham and Winder for fictional purposes. When I was a boy I never heard the name Nodoroc. Folks just called it the volcano, though it wasn't shaped like a mountain, as we normally picture a volcano.

The Nodoroc was the Creek Indians' hell, home of their devil, the Wog, a black animal with forked tongue and burning red eyes. It was some four acres of smoking, boiling, bluish mud the consistency of molasses, and sometimes a blue flame danced over its surface, which was two or three feet below the surrounding land. A column of blue smoke might rise a quarter-mile into the sky from its pocked face.

The Creeks executed their enemies and criminals by flinging them into the fiery lake, where they joined the bad spirits who had preceded them. If the Nodoroc was extremely active they might offer an innocent person as a sacrifice to appease the Wog. The Creeks captured nine Cherokees at the battle of Radoata, and it was into the fiery Nodoroc for the unfortunates, whose screams stunned a band of white settlers who happened to be in the vicinity at that instant.

Umausauga was a prominent Indian who sold eight thousand acres, including the land that Statham occupies, to the whites. He himself cast an enemy into the Nodoroc. A Choctaw warrior named Watleskew fell in love with Nere Nara, who was Umausauga's beloved. She rebuffed Watleskew, so he drove his tomahawk into her head. Umausauga, his brother Etohautee, and Nere Nara's brother Notha Neva, tracked down Watleskew and buried two tomahawks in his skull and one into his heart. Umausauga ripped out Watleskew's heart and fed it to a wolf, then he flung the body into the blue flames of hell.

Umausauga said he wanted to sell the land because of the presence of the Nodoroc. "White man afraid of it not. Indian is afraid to go. To sell it that is why devil there lives. Great Spirit is not there."

A white man named John Gossett cleared a field that nearly surrounded the Nodoroc. One morning he and his wife stood transfixed as a rumbling, gigantic eruption blasted the hot mud of the Nodoroc so thoroughly into the sky that the face of the sun was said to be darkened. The lake settled down several feet and cooled off, and it became an annoying cow mire.

There really isn't much to see nowadays. The last time I was at the Nodoroc, more than twenty-five years ago, there were malnourished trees and lots of healthy ferns on the acreage. There were a lot of snake holes and a lot of quartz.

The Nodoroc astounded humans long before the Creeks decided it was hell. It was probably before Christ walked the earth that an unknown people constructed a stone temple nearby. It was an equilateral triangle, each side twelve feet long and eight feet high. The floor also was of stone, and a stone altar revealed evidence of ceremonial sacrifice. Unfortunately, the temple and altar were dismantled in 1837. Governor George R. Gilmer bought the altar and moved it to his front yard in Lexington, Georgia.

I've never heard a scientific explanation of the Nodoroc. I decided to visit the geology department of the University of Georgia and ask someone, but the impractical, romantic side of me prevailed and I changed my mind. So far as I'm concerned it was simply a branch office of hell. I don't know why it went out of business, for there seems to be no shortage of candidates for induction.

WATER OAKS is the story of a fourteen-year-old boy named Chuck Ridley who moves from town to town because his father is a railroad man. He arrives in Hempstead in 1950 and throws in with three boys named Will Crider, Harvey Dunlap, and Curt Hill. Pam Wilson is Harvey's sweetheart, and Becky Roberts becomes Chuck's sweetheart. They are a tight little group who enjoy together what the small town has to offer.

There is a subplot involving a Joe McCarthy-type preacher who seizes on the Red-baiting scare of the 1950s for his own advancement. He accuses a prominent teacher of being a Communist. A weekly newspaper editor is one of the admired people in *Water Oaks*, and so are a teacher named Erin Parkinson and the school principal, Paul Barton, who is called Fesser, short for professor.

I've always said the main character in *Water Oaks* is the town itself. I intended to pay homage to Statham, and I did. The water oaks that line both sides of Broad Street gave me the title.

There isn't a happy ending. Once again Chuck Ridley has to move and leaves his friends and sweetheart in Hempstead. Several readers told me they cried when they reached the finish of the book. I was pleased the story moved them that much.

"There's still room for a happy ending in novels," an editor protested.

"There wasn't a happy ending in real life, and there won't be a happy ending in this book," I said. He rejected it.

Water Oaks was published in 1980. I had an outdoor book signing on Jefferson Street during a festival in Statham and sold many copies, to old friends and to strangers. I was delighted that Miss Sue Perkins, my favorite teacher, visited with me. It was a pleasure to personalize her book, and she later wrote me a letter telling me how much she enjoyed it. (I mentioned above that I saw my granddaddy listed as a member of the board of education on a 1915 Statham High graduation program. Miss Sue was listed as one of the graduates.)

A woman made sure she spoke loudly enough that I could hear her when she told her friend, "These writers write dirty novels about small towns and make them look terrible." I assumed she had read *Peyton Place* (purely in the interest of research, of course). *Water Oaks* isn't a dirty novel, and it makes Statham look inviting.

Water Oaks was optioned by a Hollywood production company. In such an arrangement a firm pays for the rights to a book for a specified length of time—in this case a year—in which it tries to secure financial backing for a film. No movie was made, though. *Star Wars* and *Jaws* and nudity were the rage at that time, and the exact words of the head of the firm to me were, "They didn't want to make it because it didn't have any tits, sharks, or robots." So much for my "dirty" novel.

I've been told that trying to match the characters in *Water Oaks* with real-life counterparts became quite a game in Statham. Well, let the game continue. I'll never tell. It's more fun that way.

THE SECOND OF my three novels about Hempstead-Statham is *Ivy,* which was published in 1986. I enjoy expanding my creative horizons when I sit before a typewriter. (I still write books on a 1950s Underwood manual.) In *Water Oaks* I had told the story of a white boy growing up in the South in the 1950s, and I decided I could tell the story of a black girl growing up in the South in the 1950s. Her name is Ivy Jo Anderson.

I've been asked at writers' conferences why I was brazen enough to put myself—a white man—into the mind of a black woman. I usually answer that I've written fiction about policemen, teachers, preachers, race drivers, Indians, Andrew Jackson, and the blind man Jesus healed in the ninth chapter of the Gospel of John, and I'm not any of those people. Hey, we're all in this mess together, and we share so many of the same hopes and disappointments. Pardon my immodesty, but it must have worked because *Players* magazine, a black publication, called the book "a great novel" and "simply wonderful."

Ivy is a grit-poor black girl who is orphaned as a teenager. She lives in Georgia during the days of unrelenting segregation, overcomes many hurdles—including the enmity of a white politician who practices his own brand of slavery—and becomes the first black teacher at the "white" high school.

Of course, I grew up in a segregated society. I graduated from Alexandria High School in Alabama in 1954, and I never attended an integrated school. I dropped out of (segregated) college to go into the newspaper business in 1955. I didn't work with a black person at my first four papers—the *Anniston Star*, the *LaGrange Daily News*, the *Gadsden Times*, or the *Montgomery Advertiser*. I joined the *Birmingham News* in 1961, but it was several years after that before the paper hired blacks in the editorial department. I've never had a black neighbor. I have several black friends, all of whom I met in athletics or in the newspaper business.

Looking back, it seems astounding that my boyhood was spent in a system of rigid segregation, of virtually no contact with black people, but I never thought about it at the time. It was just the way things were, and it never occurred to me to question it. When I lived in Statham the only black people I'd ever spoken a dozen words to were Bill Witherspoon, my granddaddy's porter at the depot in Lawrenceville, and Mayfield Camp, a barber in Statham. That was an interesting twist on segregation: Camp was a black man, but he cut only whites' hair at his shop in Statham. I think he owned a barber shop for blacks somewhere else, maybe in Winder, and split his time between the two, but I may be wrong about that.

My God, I don't even know where the black kids went to school. Did they have a high school? Did they have sports teams? If any blacks lived within the city limits of Statham I don't know it, but maybe they did. There was a balcony for them in the Royal Theater, but I don't recall many attending the movies. ("The only time I remember it being about full was when *Gone With the Wind* played," Gayle Mobley told me.) I would see blacks in the business district of Statham, buying groceries or farm supplies, and occasionally we'd watch a few innings of the black adults' baseball games on an outlying cow pasture field that had a big pile of rocks in the outfield, but that was about the extent of it. Ralph Ellison wrote a novel entitled *Invisible Man* about a black man seeking his identity. To me as a boy they were invisible people.

Wendell Hudson of Birmingham was the first black basketball player at the University of Alabama. He later became a coach of the Crimson Tide. I was interviewing him one day and I asked, "Wendell, what did you think about white people when you were growing up?"

"I didn't think anything about them," he answered. "I didn't know any white people." I told him I was in the same position in regard to blacks. I might as well have been asked what I thought about Icelanders.

MY THIRD HEMPSTEAD-STATHAM novel was *The Lost Sunshine*, which was published in 1994. For years I had wanted to write a novel with that title. It's from my favorite poem, "Out to Old Aunt Mary's" by James Whitcomb Riley: "Wasn't it pleasant, O brother mine / In those old days of the lost sunshine / Of youth . . ."

It's about a newspaper columnist (no, not me) whose mistakes of his youth in Hempstead still haunt him. He denied a black friend in the fashion of Peter denying Christ, and he didn't pursue the love of his life after her family moved to North Carolina in a crisis.

The Lost Sunshine was optioned to a film company, too. The head of the firm was enthusiastic about the story and his ability to secure financial backing. After a year he even renewed the option. I made a video of Statham scenes for him, suggesting it was the best place to shoot a movie. But my experience with the option on *Water Oaks* had taught me not to get my hopes up, and once again there was no film.

"Out to Old Aunt Mary's" reminds me of my aunt, Eva Smith, and I can't read the poem without choking up. Eva was a Mother Teresa in black high heels and white socks, smoking cork-tipped menthol Kools. A tiny dynamo of a woman, she felt it was her calling to take care of everyone in Statham. "I'm going to take Mrs. So-and-so to the doctor in Athens this afternoon," she'd say, and off she'd go in her sleek Studebaker on a mission of mercy. I never knew a more selfless person than Aunt Eva, who was my grandmother's sister.

She opened a charge account for me at Fannie Mae Sims's cafe. Simply out of the goodness of her heart. I could get a Double Cola, even a hamburger, and charge it to her. I knew not to abuse the privilege, and I never did. I visited her house on Broad Street several times a week. She always had canned jams and jellies, and she'd make me a sandwich and pour a glass of milk. Her tableware was depression glass, the glassware that folks got as premiums during the Great Depression.

She performed a memorable act of love one night after I had moved to Alabama. I was visiting her, and I went to walk with Wayne Holliday and Buck Manus. White buck shoes with red rubber soles were in style, and I had a brand new pair. We walked through an alley behind a pants plant, and the road caved in under me. A sewer line had broken, and I found myself standing ankle deep in human excrement.

I was heartsick. I walked to her house barefoot, tossed the shoes in the garbage can out back, and told Eva what had happened. When I woke up the next morning the white bucks were sitting on the back porch, as clean and pretty as could be. There wasn't a trace of soiling or odor. I don't know how she did it, but I know why she did it—because she was a wonderful woman who couldn't bear to see her nephew saddened over the loss of those brand new white bucks.

Eva lived in the Statham House, the home of the town's founder, John C. Statham. There's a historical marker in the front yard, but it wasn't there when Eva and her only child, Mote Smith Jr., lived there. The house originally was a log structure, but several remodelings hid its pioneer appearance, and it became a duplex.

Mote was two years old when his father, Eva's husband, Elmer Morton Smith Sr., was killed in a crash involving the bread truck that he drove and a lumber truck. She raised the boy herself. Her brother, Embre McDonald, and his wife, Lorna, lived in the other side of the duplex.

Eva's language could get pretty salty. She was abnormally ticklish, and she couldn't have been more devoted to Mote, but it was hilarious to watch Mote goose her and hear her yell, "Mote, you son of a bitch!"

Eva's daddy, William McDonald, died in 1918. A woman who was visiting during the wake had on an out-of-style dress with a long train. Every time she walked down the hall her dress snagged on splinters. Eva and Aunt

Jewel, the fun-loving sisters, were laughing at the sight. Zelma, the serious one, told them to hush, they should be ashamed of themselves, laughing and carrying on while their father lay a corpse.

"Oh, hell, Zelma, shut up," Eva said. "If Pappa was alive he'd be right in the middle of it."

Eva liked to say she was kicked out of the local Baptist church for playing cards. Then she would defiantly proclaim, "I'll play bridge until the day I die, and nobody can stop me!"

(Checking into her supposed banishment, I realized the wisdom of something Walter Winchell, the famous columnist, once said. "Never mess up a good story by attempting to verify it." Actually, she wasn't kicked out, but she was treated shabbily, and it had nothing to do with playing cards. Her version made a much more colorful story.)

Eva died unexpectedly in her sleep when she was seventy-eight years old. I thought at the time that wouldn't be a bad way to go. Live seventy-eight years and then depart without sickness or pain. Now that I'm seventy-four, I'm not so sold on the idea.

Mote, who never married, lived in Houston, Texas, when he became a hero. He was in a parking lot at a shopping center on a 100-degree-plus day when he spotted two little children in a locked car with the windows rolled up. One was unconscious. Mote went into the store and told the manager they had to do something. The manager got a hammer but said, hesitantly, "We'll get in trouble."

"Hell, give me the hammer," Mote said, and he ran outside and knocked out a window of the car.

The police came, and the unconscious child was whisked away to the hospital. Somehow, in the confusion, they didn't take the other one.

"I took her home with me," Mote said. "I had her all afternoon. I made diapers out of towels. Her daddy came and got her in the late afternoon."

Her mother's excuse? "I was just in the store a few minutes."

Chapter 13

When I was a kid I had an ongoing problem with boils. One day a boil on my arm became, as the saying goes, as sore as a boil. I hopped on my bicycle and rode a mile or two out Highway 29 to a doctor's house.

He examined the boil, went into his kitchen, got a slice of salt pork from the refrigerator, and bandaged it to the boil. The meat drew the boil to a head, and in a day or two I picked it with a needle and mashed the core out. He didn't charge me anything.

Fifty-five years later, while blowing out the gutters of my house in Trussville, I got a speck in my eye. It was miniscule, but that was part of the problem. I couldn't see it in the mirror without my glasses, and with my glasses on I couldn't get it out. It was mildly annoying, but I wasn't desperate, and I decided to wait a couple of hours until my wife got home and let her remove it.

But then I feared it might somehow scratch my eyeball, so I went to an optometrist I'd never seen before, figuring he'd remove the thing in five seconds and that would be that. Instead, the receptionist had me fill out a lengthy questionnaire, then the doctor looked at my eye with a magnifying contraption, fished out the speck with a Q-tip, squirted an antibiotic into my eye—and charged me a hundred bucks.

Life was indeed simple when I lived in Statham. Of course, I realize that nostalgia is selective. That's the great thing about it. I can remember a kindly doctor making me well with a slice of salt pork from his kitchen and forget the shadow of polio that darkened the South and closed swimming pools and movie theaters and caused me to be quarantined in North Carolina where I was visiting my cousins. It had the cruelest name—infantile paralysis—and everybody knew somebody who was crippled from it—or had died from it. Why, the recent president, Franklin Delano Roosevelt, was a polio victim.

But, for the most part, life really was simpler. My little dog, Scooter, was a low-maintenance fellow. A dollar for an annual rabies shot kept him in high gear. Fast forward to modern times and here I am spending more than a thousand bucks over a two-year period on a dachshund named Nascar who, I was told, should have a pharmacopeia of shots and who energetically answered the siren song of every female pooch below the Mason-Dixon Line who got in heat, no matter if the competitors for her affection were German shepherds, pit bulls, Rottweilers, leopards, crocodiles, or black mambas. Another dog with sharp teeth and jaws of massive torque castrated him—literally—but even that didn't quench his ardor. If he could have spoken I think Nascar would have said, "Well, after all, dachshunds were bred to fight badgers under ground. You wouldn't want me to be a coward, would you?" To which I would have answered, "Yes, I would."

FANNIE MAE SIMS's cafe in Statham was a simple accessory in our lives, a storefront eatery with an old tin ceiling pressed into geometric designs and a linoleum-covered counter, but the aroma of the hamburgers sizzling on the grill was magnetic, and the milkshakes were impeccable. Never mind that when Fannie Mae gazed into a shard of mirror nailed to the wall and brushed her hair she was intriguingly close to being directly over the shiny metal milkshake cup. We lived by the proverb that you had to eat a peck of dirt before you died, anyway.

Fannie Mae treated us with what could best be called benevolent disdain. She called the boys by their last names. "You need some hot chocolate, Manus. You look like you're about froze to death." "You want to move that bicycle off the sidewalk, Bolton? It would be nice if the customers didn't break their necks trying to get in here." Then she'd sculpt an extra large hamburger patty because she thought Jimmy Lowe needed to gain weight. Our hanging-out quotient exceeded our purchasing quotient, which probably was nettlesome for her, but that could be said of some adults, too. We got along with Fannie Mae, and she got along with us. If, indeed, it takes a village to raise a kid, she did her part in raising us.

Fannie Mae's had the town's only jukebox. Drop in a nickel and hear Hank Williams wailing "I'm So Lonesome I Could Cry," Mel Torme warning about "Careless Hands," Doris Day lilting about the "Bluebird on Your Windowsill." The music had actual words you could understand, and the artists weren't hideously tattooed, and they wore shirts, and they didn't bite the heads off bats and set their guitars on fire. Such pieces as "The Tennessee Waltz," "Mona Lisa," "Bouquet of Roses," "Some Enchanted Evening," "Blue Christmas, "Faraway Places," "Harbor Lights," "Dear Hearts and Gentle People," "Because of You," and "Bewitched, Bothered and Bewildered" were standard fare, and they've stood the test of time. If you wanted livelier there was always "The Huckle Buck" or "Chattanooga Shoe Shine Boy" or "If I Knew You Were Comin' I'd've Baked a Cake." Rock and roll, thank God, hadn't infected the music scene. The U.S. knew what it was doing when it played unrelenting rock music to drive Panamanian thug Manuel Noriega out of his hideout in 1989.

I can't recall any of the boys ever dancing in Fannie Mae's cafe. I know I didn't. I had zero confidence in my dancing, and it increased just a few digits over the years. I have never been a good dancer because I concentrate too much on the steps, even counting under my breath. Just go with the music is the standard advice, but there's no rhythm in my bones or brain or wherever it's supposed to be. The girls did dance with each other in Fannie Mae's, probably hoping one of us males would cut in, but I don't think we ever did.

Next door to Fannie Mae's cafe was Wirt Chambers's grocery store, a favorite haunt of the town's cracker-barrel philosophers. The downtown district was confined to Jefferson Street and Railroad Street, and there were perhaps a dozen businesses, ranging from a service station to a lumber business to an ancient hotel that finally just caved in. Wirt was a short man with a startling basso profundo voice. You wondered how anything that deep could come from a vessel that small. We kids were fascinated by the talk that Wirt and Fannie Mae, neither of whom had ever married, were sweethearts. You mean middle-aged people could be sweethearts? The town was charmed when they eventually became husband and wife.

"Rose Marie Herrin and I used to sit in Wirt's car and listen to the 'Grand Ole Opry' every Saturday night," Emma Lou Owens told me. "We'd go to the movies and see those old cowboy films and then get in Wirt's car and listen to the 'Grand Ole Opry.' Wirt didn't even know we were doing it."

FANNIE MAE'S WAS across Jefferson Street from the Royal Theater, and I kept watch through the cafe's expansive plate glass window, waiting for my sweethearts, first Gayle Mobley and later Harriette Robertson, to buy their tickets and go inside. Then I'd join them. I didn't want the woman in the booth to maybe tear off two tickets with the expectation I was paying for both.

The movies of the day weren't profane or pornographic like the garbage that is spread over screens today. A sampling: *Adam's Rib*, *The Secret Life of Walter Mitty*, *The Babe Ruth Story*, *Joan of Arc* (I was secretly in love with Ingrid Bergman), *The Treasure of the Sierra Madre*, *Red River*, *All the King's Men*, *Battleground*, *The Champion*, and *Father of the Bride* (I was darned sure secretly in love with eighteen-year-old Elizabeth Taylor). Sunset Carson, Whip Wilson, the Durango Kid, Lash LaRue, Gene Autry, Bob Steele, Roy Rogers, and Red Barry were among the riding-shooting-fighting cowboys of Saturday B flicks.

But while we were handholding in the audience, the handwriting was on the wall. On May 26, 1959, Film Daily reported that U. S. motion picture attendance dropped to an estimated average of seventy million per week in 1949, the lowest figure since 1934—and twenty-nine million a week below 1948's average. Television sets were blooming over America like jonquils, and small-town theaters were doomed. Before the 1950s ended there was no more Royal Theater.

The brick structure became the Statham fire department, but in recent years it was remodeled into an attractive civic center. When Statham High students of the 1950s gathered in the building in 2006 I was overwhelmed by memories of good times within those very walls.

In those days there was no stack of a hundred ready-cut Christmas trees waiting in the parking lot of some home improvement store—because there was no home improvement store. I suppose some trees were for sale somewhere, but most Statham families cut their own. They'd explore the abundant woods in search of a tree, or maybe they'd spot one in the summer while driving by a field and file its location in their memory. We tried for cedars, but one year I found a shapely little pine in the pasture behind our house, and for decades afterward, when the conversation turned to Christmas past, Mother marveled at how a pine tree was one of the prettiest trees we ever had.

Perry's Pond was first in our hearts, but sometimes we swam in a real swimming pool. Some church moms took a bunch of boys and girls to the Legion Pool in Athens one day, and I saw Harriette Robertson in a swimsuit for the first time. She was amused thirty years later when I remembered it was yellow. Sometimes Chick Bragg and Wayne Holliday and Jimmy Lowe and Buck Manus and I would hitchhike to Winder and swim in the city pool. They played Teresa Brewer's recording of "Music! Music! Music!" over and over again. From time to time Winder boys would give the Statham interlopers the eye and remark to each other about our presence, but we never had a problem with them. Good, because we were vastly outnumbered.

(Incidentally, Chick Bragg's name was Devant. Shortly before his death I asked him how he acquired his nickname. "When I was a little fellow and I ran, my head wobbled like a chicken's. That's what they claimed. After all these years a lot of people still call me Chick." I remember when he used to cluck-cluck-cluck and do a chicken dance when we were kids to validate his nickname.)

ONE OF OUR simple pleasures was regularly checking out the tombstone of Florence May Sanderson in the town cemetery. It is unlike any other tombstone I've ever seen, for although it appears to be of rough stone, it is made of cast iron, and it is hollow. On one side the iron is molded into a startling likeness of Florence May's thin, haunting (no pun intended) face. Having it cast must have cost a fortune. She was born on October 28, 1870, in Canton, Ohio, and she died in Statham on December 7, 1895. She was a member of a band of Northerners known as the Ohio Colony who settled in Statham.

Plates on the sides of the tombstone were held on by bolts, and they were easily removed. Legend had it that Florence May's mother, Mary Knox Sanderson, would write notes to her daughter and place them inside the tombstone, then the dead woman would answer her mother with notes of her own. Now, our little gang didn't really believe this, but we felt duty bound to occasionally unbolt the plates and peer inside. Of course, we never saw any notes or anything else from beyond the veil. I wonder if Statham kids still perform this ritual. Probably not. They've got video games instead.

Even our sins were simple, such as my snuff-dipping caper when I was in the eighth grade. One day residents of Statham opened their post office boxes and found sample cans of snuff. I believe the brand was Peach, but I'm not certain. I picked up our mail, and I stuck the snuff in my pocket and never mentioned it to my parents. A gentlewoman opened her box and frowned at the contents. I asked her if I could have her sample, and she contributed to the delinquency of a minor by handing it over.

Armed with two cans of snuff, I walked across the street and, under the depot platform, slipped a load under my bottom lip, as I had seen my grandmother, Netta Bolton, do. It took my breath, but I toughed it out. And, of course, I became nauseated and threw up.

I offered the snuff that was left to my grandmother, but she said she didn't like that brand because it was too sweet. In other words, it wasn't strong enough. It was strong enough for me, and I poured it out, careful to stand upwind.

On the trip to the 1951 state basketball tournament in Macon an older, but still underage, boy persuaded an adult to buy him a fifth of Mogen David blackberry wine. (Now that wasn't kosher, no matter what the label said.) Standing on a street corner, a bunch of us passed it around. There was maybe one decent slug per boy, not enough to make a canary slur its song, but I affected a slight stagger anyhow. I shudder when I consider how many kids of that age today not only are using drugs but are addicts.

Some members of our little gang played penny poker in an abandoned railroad section house, using apple crates for furniture. We sneered like Humphrey Bogart and Edward G. Robinson, but we never let out of our sight the card on which the ranking of the hands was printed because nobody could remember which was higher, a straight or a flush.

One day a couple of the guys were in a shed behind Chick Bragg's house when a lovely young woman and her husband drove up and got out of their car. I don't remember who the boys were. I wasn't one, and Chick said he didn't recall being one. Anyway, a yellow jacket flew up the woman's skirt and stung her, and her husband lifted the skirt to shoo the thing away. Then he wet some tobacco from a cigarette with his saliva and pressed it against the welt on her thigh to draw out the venom. The fellows in the shed saw her white panties. This wasn't some photo in a surreptitious magazine. It wasn't panties hanging on a clothesline. It was live! A woman's panties on a woman. The boys told the story, and all who heard it envied them. I asked them to tell it again, in more detail this time.

ON SUNDAY I sought forgiveness for my sins at the Statham Baptist Church. It was a stately white wooden building that was constructed in 1904. We members were proud in 1950 when an annex of eight Sunday school rooms was added. Sometimes I would enter the church during the week and talk to God and reflect on my life. Churches were never locked in those days. You could walk in any church any time. Nowadays they have to be locked because drug addicts would steal the sound systems. Dope fiends took the copper out of two central air conditioning units at my church, Taylor Memorial United Methodist in Trussville, and sold it. The copper brought only a few bucks, but the repair bill was $3,500 on each unit. (I know "dope fiend" is an antiquated term but I like it because it is so accurate. Dope does indeed transform decent people into fiends.)

We kids, uninformed by cable TV, were naïve in many ways. One late night I was awakened by the faint sound of "Rock of Ages" coming from outside the house. Maybe the preacher had preached on Revelation that Sunday, because I feared the mysterious music was ushering in the end of the world. I went to my parents' bedroom and shook Daddy's arm. We went outside and spotted a sound truck that was riding up and down Broad Street, advertising an upcoming revival.

J. R. Meek was the pastor of the Statham Baptist Church. I remember his sermons as quietly inspiring. He lived in Atlanta and, I think, was employed by one of the agencies that sprang from the Roosevelt presidency. Mother said you just knew he was a wonderful man because he drove from Atlanta to preach for a modest salary. I was, however, afflicted with an overriding impatience on Sunday mornings, and despite the admonishments of Wayne Holliday I regularly cast furtive glances at my watch. The baseball diamond, the basketball court, and Perry's Pond crooked their tempting forefingers at us, like subversive demons from a C. S. Lewis book.

NEXT TO BASKETBALL, baseball was our obsession. I was a substitute on the Statham High basketball squad in the ninth grade, but I was the regular first baseman in baseball. American Legion junior baseball was big at the time, and when the high school season ended we played for Joseph P. Harris Post 163, and I was a starting outfielder. I remember being issued brand new legion uniforms. The gray wool shirt and pants were trimmed in royal blue piping, the socks were royal blue with white stripes, and the cap was navy blue with a round gold emblem. In 1951 I batted .400 for the American Legion team.

I remember playing in an American Legion tournament on a poorly lighted field in Buford, and one of the teams had a female outfielder. Feminism might not have been a major force in the early 1950s, but it existed.

I suffered the most serious injury of my life in a baseball game. Statham High was playing Duluth High in a tournament in Duluth in 1951. The batter hit a ball to our third baseman, who threw the ball low and wide at first base. I was trying to pick up the ball in the baseline when the runner's knee caught me under the chin. I was stunned, and I stumbled off the diamond, wondering what in the world had happened, and sank to my knees. Blood was pouring from my mouth, and I couldn't speak intelligibly. A front tooth was knocked out, and other teeth were cracked.

My parents were at the game, and they rushed me to Joan Glancy Hospital in Duluth where I heard a young doctor say, "His jaw is broken. The some thing happened to me when I played football at Furman University." He sent me on to Grady Hospital in Atlanta. It turned out that my jaw was broken in two places. They wrapped a wire around each tooth, shaped them into hooks and slipped tiny rubber bands over them to hold my jaw rigid. I had to wear the wires for several weeks.

The doctor explained in World War II they wired servicemen's teeth together, without the rubber bands. Some became airsick on the flights back to the U.S. and drowned in their own vomit. At least in an emergency I could force an opening and I wouldn't drown. Better if I kept a pair of scissors on a string around my neck at school, he said, and I could cut the rubber bands. Fat chance of me going to school with scissors hanging around my neck. Jimmy Lowe and Wayne Holliday and Chick Bragg and Buck Manus would have loved that. And Stanley Pentecost probably would have cut the buttons off my shirt. I remember that it took an eternity for me to get any treatment in Atlanta. Mother fretted and Daddy fussed and I hurt as I waited in a wheelchair in the Grady Hospital emergency room while they patched up what I later learned was the usual Saturday night cast of the shot, stabbed, and clubbed. Domestic fights and differences of opinion in the blind tiger hooch joints kept the doctors busy. It was a scene I would see repeated many times in other hospitals when I was a police reporter.

They sent me home that night, and the next day my head was as big as a basketball. I remembered that Frank Sinkwich played football for the University of Georgia with a broken jaw, and I tried to draw encouragement from his example. But I wasn't Frank Sinkwich. I was a ninth grader who was seriously, painfully injured.

The next day some members of the Duluth baseball team, including the boy whose knee did the damage, came to see me. I thought that was nice. Mother served us soft drinks. I sipped mine through a glass straw that entered my mouth where the front tooth used to be. I had only liquid nourishment through the straw for several weeks—and I gained five pounds, largely through inactivity. The doctor said it was just as well the tooth was knocked out because he would have had to pull one to insert the straw. Talk about groping for a silver lining.

Frankly, I enjoyed the attention of the Statham kids and adults. I saw myself as a wounded warrior fallen for the glory of dear old SHS. After I shed the wires and rubber bands I regarded the space where the deleted incisor had been as a badge of honor. I wasn't in the least reluctant to smile. It was a couple of years before I got—or wanted—a bridge to fill the gap. I still have some of the get-well cards, including one from Gayle Mobley.

I was injured in the early spring, and I returned to play on the American Legion junior team that summer. At first I was afraid to stand in against a high curve ball, even though I knew it would break away from me. The last thing I needed was a baseball hitting me in the face. But I quickly conquered that fear, and I enjoyed a good season.

I had a first baseman's mitt that wouldn't stand up. It was limp. I sold it to Jimmy Lowe, who succeeded me as the Statham High first baseman after I moved away. I'll let him tell the story, as he did to me in 2007:

"Do you remember that old first baseman's mitt I bought from you? It flopped over. I got two pieces of thick leather from a shoe shop, and they held it up. One was in the thumb, the other in the other part. I was the first baseman for the high school, and I was chewing Day's Work tobacco. Somebody threw a ball, and the lacing on that mitt was rotten, and the ball went right through it and hit me on the Adam's apple, and I swallowed that tobacco. Mr. Barrett said, 'Take him over in that shade. He'll be all right.'"

Jimmy, incidentally, enjoyed a privilege that was beyond the other boys in our little gang. He was a member of the Athens YMCA. He was on the boxing team, and swam and played basketball and even football. In fact, he played football with Fran Tarkenton, the future Georgia quarterback who reached the halls of fame of both college and professional football. Jimmy would hitchhike to Athens and back, or maybe if it was raining he'd spend twenty cents to ride the bus. "It was a different time," he spoke our familiar refrain. "You didn't think anything about sticking out your thumb and hitchhiking to Athens."

If we weren't playing baseball for the American Legion junior team in the summer we were watching the Statham town team, which also was sponsored by the American Legion post and which we called the "Big Legion." The adult team played in the Independent League. Townspeople would bring their chairs and sit on the hill behind the third base line on the school diamond and watch Statham face rivals Athens, Farmington, Bogart, Diamond Hill, Watkinsville, Colbert, Comer, Monroe Mills, and Walton Mills on Saturday and Sunday afternoons.

Johnny Fincher was a long drink of water at first base. He must have been six-feet-five or taller. Pete Holliday, the pitcher, was called Peter the Hermit because he frequently had a beard of two weeks' growth, this in a time when men didn't wear beards. (I didn't know until decades later that Peter the Hermit was a French monk who was an instigator of the First Crusade and who appeared in an ancient poem, so Pete Holliday must have been nicknamed by someone who knew history or arcane poetry.) I admired the third baseman, Junior Sheats, who smiled confidently even as he snagged a bouncing ball, knowing the runner had no chance of beating his throw across the diamond. A shortstop nicknamed Suction Mac (was it McDonald or McDaniel?) vacuumed up every ball hit near him. I don't remember the manager's name but, man, he had a presence. He wore aviator sunglasses and smoked cork-tipped Kools, and he never got rattled and he never smiled. When I was the batboy I was proud to hold the army surplus bag open while he stuffed the bats inside. But my favorite Big Legion warrior was the catcher, Dick Steed, who eschewed all the customary protections of his office except the mask.

Bill Barrett, Bill Crowe, and Jimmy Perkins were older boys who sometimes played with the Big Legion (Barrett stationed in left field with his Trapper model first baseman's mitt), and I visualized myself as one day being on the roster. I never was, because we moved from Statham before I entered the tenth grade, but as a teenager I played for a couple of town teams in Alabama and in one game miraculously hit a home run, a triple, two doubles, and a single.

We competed for the job of batboy for the Big Legion because the batboy was the recipient of any cracked bat or ball with unraveling stitches. We'd try to arrive earlier than our pals and secure the manager's guarantee of batboyhood. There were no aluminum bats in those days. They were made of wood, and a favorite was the Hanna Batrite, which was manufactured right there in Athens. Bats usually splintered just above the handle. We'd drive a couple of small nails into the thing, wrap it in sticky black friction tape, and it was good to go. We patched baseballs with friction tape, too, and if a horsehide was beyond salvation we'd rip it off and cover the entire ball with tape. We kept a ball on life support as long as possible. Today, when I walk at the youth sports complex in Trussville, I frequently find perfectly good baseballs that were fouled or homered over fences. Nobody even bothers to go get them.

The Big Legion's road games were torture on us young fans. The thought of the team playing in another town while we stayed in Statham was excruciating. The adult players gathered at the American Legion hall on Jefferson Street and left in a caravan. Wayne Holliday, Jimmy Lowe, Chick Bragg, Buck Manus, and I would show up, hoping to bum a ride in one of the cars. I can still hear those dread words—"Sorry, all full"—that meant I would spend Sunday afternoon at home.

The American Legion also sponsored a men's basketball team. One year some University of Georgia football players, including All-America quarterback Johnny Rauch and future all-NFL tailback Joe Geri, formed a basketball squad and played town teams in the area. It was supposed to be all in fun, and they tried to do a football-themed version of the Harlem Globetrotters' act. (Geri attempted to kick a field goal), but the Statham players took it seriously, and a free-for-all broke out on the floor. A huge fat man who was sitting with my parents declared, "I'm going to get some of that," and despite his wife's hysterical pleas he charged out of the stands and onto the court. One of the football players immediately zeroed in on his necktie and began choking him with it. The fat man's eyes were threatening to pop out of his skull when the Bulldog released the garrote and kicked him in the butt and off the court, the civilian's enthusiasm for combat at an end.

In addition to basketball and baseball squads, Statham High had a track team. As a freshman in 1951 I won the hundred-yard dash at the Ninth District meet on the University of Georgia campus, and Statham won the team championship. Merely running on the Georgia track was a big deal to me, and winning made it that much more satisfying. It was like most tracks of that day in that the surface was of cinders from institutional furnaces. Trackmen wore shoes with sharp spikes that were perhaps an inch long. The cinders were held in place by concrete curbs—which also tended to hold in rainwater. My time in the hundred that day? I'll never tell. I'll just quote the yellowed clipping from an Athens newspaper that I still have: "Sprint and distance times were not exceptional because of rain that threatened until the last minute to postpone the meet."

I was also a member of the winning 880-yard relay team, and I finished second in the 220-yard dash to a Maysville runner named Reynolds. Or at least the judge said I did. I thought that day that I won that race, and I still think I did. I wish there had been a camera at the finish line.

WE HAD SOMETHING that city kids couldn't match, our own amusement park in the guise of the Seaboard depot. Daddy's depot was the center of Statham, figuratively and literally. The city limits of the village, founded by Englishman J. C. Statham, extended one mile in every direction from the depot. The coming of the Georgia, Carolina and Northern Railway Company in 1890–91 marked the evolution of Statham from the location of a few houses into a real town. The first depot was built around 1900 and the present one in 1912.

When I lived in Statham, streamliners with their silver cars stopped and took on passengers, then sped romantically away. I made up stories about the people who gazed from the windows while others got on board, all the while the train straining and making impatient snorts and wheezes like some monster sprinter in the blocks. The freight trains, on the other hand, were blue-collar vehicles of commerce, bringing goods in, taking goods out, emptying and filling the freight room, and diminishing the scores of cotton bales that overflowed the depot's platform and stretched up Railroad Street when cotton was king.

We kids leaped from bale to bale, with no purpose other than the joy of it, and when there was no cotton we rode our bikes around and around on the platform, dangerously near the edges, and then at full pedal shot down the ramp that emptied into the street.

Daddy occasionally let me hand up the orders to the speeding trains with "train sticks." They were limbs—willow, I suppose—bent to the shape of a "9" and seasoned to hardness. The order was clipped to the stick, and a member of the train crew held out his arm in a crook. As the train whizzed by, he hooked the train stick, quickly removed the order, and tossed the stick beside the track. It took courage to stand near the train and not flinch, but I wanted to prove to Daddy I could do it, and I never failed.

But the trains don't stop in Statham anymore. The depot where my granddaddy and daddy were agents is still there, owned by Kurt Bogenrieder, who moved from New York state nineteen years ago to work at the University of Georgia. "I've always played with old things," he told me in 2007. "I've always been a collector."

He bought the depot at a sealed auction in 1999. "I didn't really have any plans for it at the time. I just thought it was the thing to do. It's the most prominent building downtown."

He and his wife, Christine, repaired the depot and opened an antique shop, Along the Line, which is appropriate for such a historical building.

I drop by when I'm in Statham and gaze at the bay window in front of the building where my daddy sat, writing orders for the Silver Comet, the passenger train that has long since streaked into history.

I am pleased the depot is in the hands of a man and woman who appreciate it. I am less confident of its immortality when Kurt tells me, "We own the building, but we don't own the real estate under it." The CSX railroad corporation owns the land. Kurt bought the building with the knowledge that someday it might have to be torn down or moved, but that was eleven years ago, and it still stands. "I don't worry about it happening," he said. "If it does, it does; if it doesn't, it doesn't."

Hang in there, old depot.

Chapter 14

Statham High School died in 1956, and the older townspeople mourn it even today, as they would mourn any old friend who nurtured them and helped sculpt their characters and embraced them while they laughed and loved. It has been dead for more than half a century—longer than it lived, actually—but I still mourn it.

Some parliamentarians would take issue with my statement that Statham High School died. Officially, it was consolidated with Winder High School to form Winder-Barrow High School. The last graduation exercise of Statham High was held on June 1, 1956, and the town was left with only an elementary school. No more would the Statham High Wildcats in their red satin jerseys race up and down the basketball court and destroy opponents from higher classifications. No more would graduates of their hometown school flip their tassels at commencement exercises. No more would daydreaming students gaze out the second-floor windows of the brick building that was constructed in 1907 and see forever—because Statham High not only died on paper, it was slain by the wrecking ball.

Call it what you want, but if that ain't dying I don't know what is. What I know is that there is a high school in Winder and there isn't one in Statham, and if you live in Statham you go to high school in Winder.

No doubt apologists of consolidation could offer logical, bottom-line reasons for the execution of Statham High School, but taking a town's school rends its heart, much as taking its churches would. I was long gone, working for a newspaper in LaGrange, Georgia, when Statham High died, and I'm glad I wasn't there when the wreckers attacked. I couldn't have watched. I felt empty the first time I looked up the slight incline that had led to the tall old edifice with a cupola on top and saw only sky. I wonder what happened to the barn owls that lived in the upper reaches of the building.

My pal Jimmy Lowe's mother, Hester Lowe Booth, who taught in Statham for thirty-six years, was there when the wrecking ball knocked an enormous hole in her old classroom. "I didn't stay to watch," she said. "I couldn't keep back the tears. A lifetime of memories were piling up on the ground below."

Her memories extended beyond her first day as a teacher, for she had been a student at Statham High. She remembered when there was a well that was enclosed in a latticed building, and a dipper hung on the wall. Boys vied for the honor of drawing the water. On particularly hot days her teacher would permit a bucket of water in the classroom. Students had their individual cups or they folded sheets of tablet paper to hold water.

She remembered silver maples that lined the walkway from the street to the school when she was six years old. She remembered a massive oak that spread its limbs like a circus big top. She and her schoolmates gathered under the tree and pitched horseshoes and sang the popular songs of the day, and she reckoned some romances got their start there. My schoolmates and I were sheltered by the same oak a generation later. It, too, became a victim of the mischief of "progress." It was murdered in 1974 to make room for classrooms.

THERE WERE THREE buildings when I attended the eleven-grade school in Statham in 1948–51.

The crown jewel, the one that was destroyed in 1956, was indeed a two-story structure, but the ceilings were high enough that it could have accommodated three floors. There had been a gymnasium on the second floor. The gym already had been partitioned into classrooms when I was a student, but the markings of the basketball court were still visible on the floor. It was the first all-brick school building in Barrow County, and it was a beauty, no kin to the featureless, fundamental school structures of today. There was lots of brick trimming outside, including arches over the upstairs windows. The entrance stood out from the main body, creating an appearance of depth and stateliness. The intricate roof slanted from front to back and from side to side. A brigade of chimneys bespoke the era in which it was constructed. The town passed a bond issue of $8,000 to erect the building, and a high school was started in 1907, with the first graduating class in 1909. There were three members of that class, all girls—Sara Lowe, Viola Arnold, and Myron Guinn. At first there were only nine grades. The tenth was added in 1913, the eleventh in 1922, and the twelfth in 1952.

Hester Lowe Booth returned to Statham High after college for the life of a small-town teacher. One of her duties was taking up the price of admission to basketball games in the old second-floor gymnasium, which also served as an auditorium. She recalled that it was seldom over a quarter. There were bleachers on each side of the court and a pot-bellied stove at each end. The students' cheering section was on the stage. Teachers were required to be at the games, if not to take up money, to be scattered throughout the place to maintain order.

It was a modest gym, but Statham was proud of it. Its predecessor was an outdoor court, and besides, some other schools were playing basketball in abandoned store buildings. Money was tight in Georgia.

An L-shaped one-story brick building that housed the grammar grades, the library, the auditorium, and the principal's office and that eventually would be the centerpiece of the Statham school triad was built in 1927, and a brick gymnasium was constructed in 1942.

I'm told the high school building had become unsafe. That didn't make its death any more palatable. If a favorite uncle was terminally ill, you'd still be sad when he drew his last breath. After its destruction they bobtailed the middle building by knocking off much of the back and added a couple of nondescript one-story structures to the complex. One, incredibly, blocks the view from the street of the gorgeous old middle building and its dramatic arched doorways. A recent $8 million construction-renovation project provides necessary expansion, but the school is merely utilitarian and not a thing of beauty as it once was.

When I was a student in the old high school building I was made acutely aware of how a fraction of an inch, a fraction of a second, can change lives. I was standing on a second-floor balcony in the back. I held an empty Coca-Cola bottle over the railing, between my thumb and forefinger, and aimed at a spot on the ground. It was one of those thick, heavy ones that you see in antique stores today. I dropped it, and at that moment my basketball teammate Jack Cook stepped out the first-floor back door. The Coke bottle barely nipped the tip of his nose as it plummeted to the ground.

He was startled and I was speechless, but he wasn't injured. The slightest variation in circumstances and his nose would have been broken. His skull could have been fractured. He could have been killed. Thank you, Lord.

When I was there the bricks of the old building had faded to orange in the punishing heat of so many Georgia summers. A long, wide, sturdy banister that accompanied the staircase between floors had acquired a patina appropriate to its age. We loved to ride that thing when classes changed, to the consternation of the teachers. Here would come a covey of students walking up the steps and some adventurer (I plead guilty) sliding down the banister at speed. It reminds me of those police chases on TV in which the fleeing criminal drives against the traffic and everyone tries to get out of the way. Mr. Barrett, the principal, issued dire prohibitions against riding the banister, but fellow students wouldn't rat us out.

WHY IS IT that the stern, no-nonsense teachers are the ones we remember most fondly? Because we know they were right and had our best interests at heart? Such a one was Clarence Thomas, who taught science at Statham. He was minister of a local Christian church to boot, and he did not suffer fools gladly.

He not only looked you straight in the eye, he raised his chin a tad, and that visage warned you that he had heard it all, and your excuses might as well crawl from your lips back into your conniving mind without articulation. I could pass my schoolwork with little effort, and I became content making grades that were well below what a conscientious approach would have produced. Mr. Thomas asked me to stay after class one day, and he placed my open report card on his desk. "You could do so much better than this," he said, "It's so disappointing when a student with a bright mind like yours is content to be mediocre. It's a shame."

That's all he said. That's all he had to say. I got on the ball and jacked my grades back up to an acceptable level.

Not every scene at Statham High was painted by Norman Rockwell.

I said Mr. Thomas didn't accept excuses. One time he did, but I thought it showed Christian mercy to do so, because he had a student over a barrel—I mean over a desk. We had those old oak desks with a folding seat and a round hole in the top where an inkwell had been, but the inkwells had long been removed. It was between classes, and Stanley Pentecost, who delighted in the role of class clown more than anyone I knew before or since, began cooing to a desk as it if were a pretty girl. Several of us boys were his audience, and when we laughed that was all the encouragement he needed. He unzipped his pants and—well, you can guess the rest.

Who should enter the room but Mr. Thomas, the dread reverend. Stanley was draped over the desk with his back to the teacher and couldn't see him. The rest of us saw him, though, and fell silent and wiped the smiles off our faces. "What. Are. You. Doing. Stanley?" Mr. Thomas said in his best Jehovah timbre.

Stanley was trapped. He couldn't stand up. He couldn't turn to face Mr.

Thomas. He was speechless for what seemed an eternity, then you could almost see the words trembling in the air as he said, "I'm looking for my pencil. I dropped my pencil."

Mr. Thomas let him stew in silence for maybe fifteen more seconds, then he said, "Find it and get to class," and he walked away. I suppose he thought Stanley had suffered enough.

Stanley's main target was Mrs. Evelyn Harris, the same teacher whose tires he deflated. One day she sentenced him not only to sit in the corner but to be exiled from the rest of the class by a large folding screen. So there we were, Stanley behind the screen, the screen to the teacher's back, and the teacher facing the class. Stanley tossed up a wad of paper and caught it. We covered our mouths and tried not to laugh. Again the paper went up and down. And again, and again, and again. The teacher turned around to see what was going on. Stanley could see through the crack that separated sections of the screen, and he stopped tossing the paper. Mrs. Harris turned to face the class, and the tossing resumed. This comedy went on and on and on. It was well remembered, for it was a topic of conversation in 2006 at a reunion of Statham High students of the 1950s.

Mrs. Harris came from Winder, and that was a strike against her. Make that two strikes. Chick Bragg wasn't referring to Mrs. Harris, but he spoke the truth succinctly more than half a century later when he said, "Winder was a foreign place as far as Statham was concerned." Mrs. Harris spent much of her time putting out brush fires of insubordination.

Emma Lou Owens and Gayle Mobley remembered the day Lulu scattered Mrs. Harris's home economics class. (We always called her Lulu. She doesn't remember how it got started. "I've dropped Lulu now," she told me, "and now people just call me Lou.")

"The plumbing was torn up in the kitchen part of the school," Emma Lou told me. "You remember the kitchen part, don't you? They had a hose, trying to flush it out, I guess."

"I slipped into the kitchen and got the hose—no, the water wasn't on—and came through the Home Ec. classroom hollering, 'Fire! Fire!'"

"Everybody was jumping up and running every which way," Gayle remembered. "Mrs. Harris thought it was a fire, too."

Mrs. Harris extinguished Lulu's flame. "I had to write about a thousand times, on paper, 'I will not do so and so.'"

She remembered another of Stanley's pranks. Stanley just couldn't resist the temptation afforded by electric sewing machines sitting idle in Home Ec. class. He'd slip in before class and turn them all on and rev them up as far as possible and slip out. "Mr. Barrett would get all over him for that," Emma Lou said.

The unkindness of kids is legendary and especially virulent in a pack. A group of students laughed one day at an FHA or 4-H camp when Mrs. Harris slipped and fell while walking down a hill. "I can't believe children would laugh about someone falling down," she said.

Gayle told me that in later years, when she was an adult and living in Winder, she'd see Mrs. Harris in the grocery store, and the teacher always greeted her. "I'd think, 'Gosh, lady, if I were you I wouldn't speak to me, as ugly as I treated you.'"

One day Mr. Thomas was grading papers, and he told the class to lay our heads on our desks and be perfectly quiet until he finished. You knew he meant perfectly quiet, and you dared not even whisper.

There was a total silence when some unfortunate soul who probably had eaten butterbeans (a staple in the Statham lunchroom) tried to discreetly relieve the pressure on his belly. It didn't work. With the seat of the wooden desk as a sounding board, the report was startling.

We tried not to laugh, we really did, but a chorus of snickers escaped. We didn't dare raise our heads or speak, but we were shaking with mirth like so many Model T Fords that had just been cranked. I couldn't see Mr.

Thomas's face, so I can't testify as to his reaction. He didn't say a word.

To this day I don't know the identity of the poor unfortunate. Nobody confessed, and none of his neighbors squealed on him. Never to miss a rich opportunity when it presented itself, some of us boys blamed it on a succession of girls, who screamed denials and tried to hit us with their school books.

The girls were our buddies, though. There was a boys' bathroom in the basement of the middle building that was accessible from outside. It was available to kids playing on the playground or to spectators watching baseball games. "I wonder what that place looks like inside," Lulu said. No one else was around, so I volunteered a guided tour.

We passed the heavy wooden door, and her eyes fell on the long homemade concrete urinal. She gazed at it for a few seconds and finally asked, "Why do they have a bathtub in here?"

There was a quirk in Mr. Thomas's dress that I'd never seen before and have never seen since. He wore white dress shirts, and his wife cut the sleeves off in the summer and sewed them back on in the winter. The overlaps were plainly visible.

Another legendary tough teacher was Miss Sue Perkins. Like so many of the female teachers of that era, she never married. Her perfectly sculpted white hair framed a face that could reflect the kindest concern for a struggling student and direst censure of a miscreant. When she was my seventh grade teacher I thought she was an old woman. In later years I did the arithmetic and realized she was just fifty years old.

Coca-Cola used to provide foot-long wooden rulers to each student, and Miss Sue used them to administer corporal punishment. An offender was required to extend his or her hand, palm up, and receive a blow. I can testify it smarted. Imprinted on the ruler was the Golden Rule: do unto others as you would have them do unto you. (Since that's biblical, I don't suppose it would be legal advice to a school child today.) I wanted to ask her if she saw the irony in hitting someone with the Golden Rule, but I didn't dare, not then and not in later adult life. Of course, she would have simply answered that if she had cut up like we did she would have hoped the teacher would punish her.

I'd see Miss Sue occasionally on my trips to Statham after I was an adult, and we'd share stories and laughs about the old days. I regretted my last visit to her side, though. She was ninety-five years old and in a home that provided care for the aged in Athens. "You can see her," the woman at the desk said, "but she won't know you." An attendant took me to her room and, indeed, she didn't know me, so I introduced myself. "I was one of your students when you were a teacher," I said. She thought I was accusing her of stealing. I kept trying to explain who I was and why I was there, but she grew more and more agitated until she was frantic. I said goodbye to my favorite teacher and drove away crying. Lord, why did I go to that place that day? Why did that have to be my last image of Miss Sue?

I TOOK VOCATIONAL agriculture at Statham High—which, incidentally, was the home of the first Future Farmers of America chapter in Georgia. I had no intention of becoming a farmer, but "Ag," as we called it, was a required subject. I think R. H. Willingham, the teacher, favored the farm boys—as he should have. He wanted to show them methods to make their work easier and more productive. There wasn't any point in teaching Wayne Holliday or Jimmy Lowe or me how to farm. God bless farmers, but don't hand me a plow. I'm talking about family farms of the 1950s, where kids had to work long and hard in the fields, alongside their parents. The farm boys wore overalls and ankle-high brogans that were stiffened by sweat and rain and mud; "iron shoes," as one of William Faulkner's fictional characters so aptly called them. Some of the farm boys already had milked the cows and gathered the eggs before they arrived at school. While the rest of us played ball after school, they chopped cotton and broke the ground in the wake of mules.

The arrival of the school buses every morning was a reminder that Statham was, indeed, a country school. The yellow transporters were dusty from their missions on dirt roads. With fingertips, students wrote their names in the pinkish overlay. They wrote "Yay Wildcats" and "Boo Bogart" and they drew hearts with their initials and those of their true loves in the center. The dust also blew inside the un-air-conditioned buses, frustrating the fastidious among the rural scholars.

Parking for the students' cars wasn't a problem at Statham High School. Not because there was plenty of space, but because the students didn't have cars. If a single pupil had an automobile, I don't remember it. Check out the parking lot at a modern high school and there are scores of vehicles driven by the scholars. Come to think of it, some families in Statham didn't have cars, and if any family had two cars, I don't know who it was.

Courage is where you find it, even on the stage of a high school auditorium in a small town. Older students were having their senior play, and one had watched a welding torch without darkened goggles that day. He was temporarily blinded. I don't remember his name, but he had a prominent part in the play, and he soldiered on in sunglasses, other members of the cast tugging on his arm and guiding him to various spots on the stage.

On the front campus we played a game we called rollabat. It was tremendously popular at recess and before school. The cast consisted of a pitcher, a batter, a catcher, and any number of fielders, none wearing gloves. The batter stayed at bat until someone caught a ball on the fly or on the first bounce or rolled the ball and hit the bat, which the batter placed at his feet. The person who succeeded in any of these three challenges then became the batter. Rolling the ball across the uneven campus was much like playing the break of a putt on a golf green. (Maybe the correct name was roll-at-the-bat, but we just said rollabat.) I doubt it was native to Statham, but I never played it anywhere else. Miss Sue Perkins's house was in front of the school, across the street, and we fantasized about hitting a ball onto her wide front porch, but since we played with softballs and rubber baseballs, no one ever did.

Sports dominated our lives. Take away TV and video games, and air conditioners and sports would dominate the lives of more boys of today, too. Glenn Jackson, a staunch citizen of Statham and a kindly man, was our scoutmaster. We met in the gymnasium, but we frequently cajoled him into simply letting us play basketball. The Boy Scout motto is "Be Prepared," and we wanted to be prepared to win basketball games, so we felt that shooting hoops instead of learning knots was justified.

THERE WAS AN old man who came to school and taught penmanship, perhaps once a week. He was not one of the regular teachers, and I don't remember his name. I think he lived in the old hotel, but I may be wrong about that. He was a dignified sort of fellow—as you'd expect a teacher of penmanship to be—but his suit and vest and tie and white shirt were, shall we say, experienced. I suspect he had seen much better days. In fanciful moments today I like to think of him as a defrocked Russian professor, and exiled confidant of the Czar, though he no doubt was never any closer to Russia than I have been.

His penmanship was, indeed, majestic. It swirled and slanted and dipped and soared. It was art. It was inspiring to watch him cross a "t." Well, not inspiring enough to make us actually practice penmanship outside the classroom. I've never known anyone in the real world to write like that. Nothing poisons your handwriting like being a reporter, and my accelerated newspaper note taking bears the same resemblance to his penmanship that bologna does to filet mignon. Do they even teach penmanship in schools anymore? Does anyone write with a pen anymore, or is it all done on computers?

School books were free, but they were passed on from one year to the next, and some were in deplorable condition. Getting your books on the first day of school could be a disappointment or a pleasant surprise or a combination of the two. It was a treat to be issued a new book, to know that no eyes except yours had seen those pages. Opening it and exercising its spine created a sound like that of dry cornhusks being separated. (When I moved to Alabama I was surprised to find school books were not free. Parents had to pay for them.)

There was a lot of making do at Statham High. In one class there weren't enough books to go around, and desks were pulled together and books shared. I was paired with Stanley Pentecost, who spent a good deal of his time trying to make me laugh. He succeeded.

I think of our little gang and those relatively innocent days and I get angry when I see television and the movies slandering the kids of the 1950s. Darrell Kent, the protagonist of *The Lost Sunshine*, my novel that is set in the fictional Hempstead, Georgia, addressed that issue:

> The fifties as you see them portrayed on television didn't exist—well, maybe in Brooklyn, New York, that was the way it was, I don't know, but it wasn't like that in Hempstead, Georgia, or anywhere else I ever went.
>
> TV is concerned with image, not truth, and its image of fifties' kids is a guy with a greasy ducktail haircut and wearing a black leather jacket and motorcycle boots and snapping his fingers and making cute remarks, and a brainless girl smacking chewing gum and idolizing him and begging to ride in his customized Mercury with red and yellow and orange flames painted on the side. TV can flash that picture, and *1950s* immediately registers in the mind of the viewer, and instead of having to invent real human beings, it can get on with what passes for a plot.
>
> I saw perhaps a half-dozen of those characters in the fifties, no more. They weren't the crowd, anymore than the idiots with purple and green hair and rings in their noses are the crowd today. They stood out from the crowd.

> The average fifties' kid was neat, polite, civilized. *He* wore short hair and clean clothes, and if he was lucky enough to drive a car it was the family Studebaker, which didn't have flames painted on the side. *She* was scrubbed and her saddle oxfords were polished, and her skirt was pressed. She didn't pride herself on her right to say "shit" every other sentence just like a man.

I agree with Darrell Kent when he says, "I think the fifties were the best possible years in which to have grown up."

Chapter 15

I don't remember who broke the bad news to me. Maybe it was Daddy, maybe it was Mother, maybe it was both of them. It didn't matter who the messenger was. What mattered was the message—that Daddy had taken another job in another town.

So once again the vagabond Boltons were on the move. Willie Nelson sang that he couldn't wait to get on the road again. The ponytailed troubadour must have been related to my parents.

The goofy thing about this upheaval was that Daddy had accepted a job as the Seaboard agent in Winder, which is just eight miles from Statham, yet he uprooted his family, body and soul. Now, if you took a job eight miles from home wouldn't you continue to live in the same town, in the same house? We didn't. We shucked the home we owned in Statham and rented one in Winder rather than afflict Daddy with a sixteen-mile commute. Hell, for the last twenty-seven years of my newspaper career I had a thirty-five-mile round trip commute.

I was devastated. I loved Statham. I loved it more than anywhere else I had ever lived. I loved our little gang. I loved skinny-dipping in Perry's Pond and slurping thick chocolate milkshakes in Fannie Mae Sims's cafe and listening at night with Wayne Holliday to the radio broadcasts of the Atlanta Crackers games and eating weenies that were roasted over a campfire. I loved being on the high school basketball, baseball, and track teams. I loved holding hands in the Royal Theater and digging fishing worms in the backyard. And now we were moving to Winder? Winder, the big school that was frequently embarrassed by little Statham's fast-breaking basketball squads?

Well, yeah, we were moving. But we weren't moving immediately. Which made the situation more confusing. We were still living in Statham when I started to Winder High School. There was no need for me to begin the tenth grade at Statham High because we were going to move in a few weeks. That didn't mean I would have a few precious afternoons left with our little gang, though. I had gone out for football at Winder, and my afternoons were consumed by practice. I rode to Winder with Daddy in the morning, attended school and football practice, and rode back to Statham with him in the evening.

I was allowed to attend Winder High while still living in Statham, but I wasn't permitted to play in a football game that season of 1951 until we moved to Winder. It was a sensible rule, of course, one that kept coaches from recruiting players from other towns. (Not that anyone would have recruited me.) So while I practiced and dressed out on game nights, I wasn't eligible to see action in the first couple of games.

The coach at Winder High had been Doc Ayers. I thought he would be my coach, but during the off-season he took a similar job at Cedartown High. (In later years, when I was a sportswriter and he was a member of Vince Dooley's University of Georgia staff, I kidded Doc that by not coaching me at Winder he missed a challenge that would have tested all his skills.)

Winder brought in Coach Joe Pope from some town in Florida, and before school started he took us to train for ten days at something called Camp Rutledge. I think the grim place had been a WPA camp during the Roosevelt administration. There was a Spartan dormitory with lumpy, creaky cots, sans air conditioning, and we rolled out at 6 A.M. and soon afterward were on the hardpan practice field for the first of two daily workouts. We did get to cool off in a lake between drills.

I didn't know anybody on the team. I was sleeping in the dorm with total strangers. I hadn't even been to school with them yet. I was competing against guys who had played on midget teams and B teams and varsity teams, and I didn't even know how to put on a uniform—literally. They made individual photos at the camp, and in mine the winged thigh pads that fit into the pockets in the front of the pants are pointing inward instead of outward. If I had been tackled in that mode I would have become an instant soprano—and I don't mean a member of the TV crime family.

Being Charley Trippi or Frank Sinkwich in Wayne Holliday's backyard didn't transfer to learning the playbook and hitting the blocking sled at Winder High. Wrestling Gayle Mobley to the ground after she caught a pass didn't prepare me to tackle Billy Ted McDaniel, Winder's fast, pulverizing running back.

Nobody wore face masks in 1951. Winder was past the leather helmet stage. Some players had modern plastic headgear and others, including me, wore hats of some composite material (we called them turtle shells). Our helmets were silver and our shirts were red, the same colors of the University of Georgia's helmets and shirts. We, too, were Bulldogs. I joke in speeches that I was so good my number (34) was retired twice—once when Herschel Walker wore it and once when Bo Jackson wore it.

Nobody asked me what position I wanted to play. Coach Pope and his assistant, Hokey Jackson, designated me a lineman, specifically a tackle. I remember vividly the first play of the first scrimmage in boot camp. I reckoned they'd give the ball to Billy Ted McDaniel, the right halfback, and send him at the new fish, the 135-pound defensive left tackle from Statham. The offensive tackle, who was fifty pounds heavier, would try to smear me. I had no doubt he could achieve said smearing, so rather than battle him head-on I decided to guess whether McDaniel would run off the tackle's inside shoulder or his outside shoulder and then try to fill that hole. If I guessed correctly I might make a play; if I guessed incorrectly

I'd look like an idiot—which is what I was going to look like anyway if I didn't guess at all.

I guessed outside shoulder, and I dropped McDaniel at the line of scrimmage. The coaches and the defensive players yelled and slapped me on the back. "Way to go, Statham," McDaniel said as he pushed himself to his feet.

It meant nothing. The offensive tackle did smear me the rest of the session. I didn't make another play. I looked like the untutored, inexperienced lost ball in high weeds that I was, and it was obvious I had merely gotten lucky on that first snap. As we walked off the field I muttered, "Boy, I'm tired."

The offensive tackle said, "Why? You didn't do nothing." He was right.

Obviously, I wasn't cut out to be a lineman, and since I was fast Coach Pope moved me to fullback and linebacker. But I was so far down the depth chart Jacques Cousteau couldn't have found me. At least I got to stand up straight and carry the ball in practice.

I got little personal attention from the coaches, and with no grasp of the fundamentals, I didn't improve. I felt alienated from them and from the other players, more like a tackling dummy than a member of the team. But from the viewpoint of an adult, I can better understand the situation. Joe Pope was about to field his first Winder High School squad. He hadn't even had the boys for spring practice. He wanted to make a splash, but he probably realized the level of material was suspect. How much time should he devote to a tenth-grader who had never played football and who wasn't even eligible for the first couple of games?

As a member of the varsity I might as well have been nailed to the bench. A B team was formed from varsity scrubs and played a few games. I wasn't even a starter on the B team. I was embarrassed, knowing that kids and adults from Statham were in the audience at Winder's games. The happy, competent athlete and popular boy from Statham High had become an anonymous, confused cipher of an athlete at Winder High.

I remember the first play I ever ran in a game. How could I forget it? The Winder B team was playing a team from the Athens YMCA. We were using the single-wing formation, and I was the fullback. The coach called a buck-lateral play. That meant the ball would be snapped to me, I would fake a plunge into the line but hand the ball to the blocking back who would lateral it to the wingback on an end run.

Instead of handing the ball to the blocking back I pitched it to him from a couple of feet away. Why? Damned if I know. He was surprised and didn't catch it, of course, and the opponents recovered the fumble. As I came off the field, Coach Jackson looked at me and then looked at the ground and shook his head. He didn't say anything. That validated my low opinion of myself, that I wasn't even worth chewing out. (A Holiday Inn is now on the ground where that game was played. I frequently stay there when I'm in Athens, and I always recall that play.)

Winder's varsity opened the season with an 86–0 victory over Cumming. I wasn't eligible to play, so I watched the massacre from the bench. I've always wondered if my Winder football experience might have been different if I could have played in that game. Maybe I would have gained some valuable experience against the marshmallow team. Maybe I could have made some decent plays, even scored a touchdown. Maybe I could have gained some confidence. But, as Dandy Don Meredith used to say on *Monday Night Football*, "If ifs and buts were candy and nuts, we'd all have a merry Christmas."

WE HAD A mediocre football team (I don't even remember our record), and I was glad when the season ground to a merciful end. I didn't even entertain the notion of playing basketball or baseball or running track at Winder. I had no friends and certainly no girlfriend at Winder High. I don't remember the name of a single student other than my teammates. I don't remember the name of any teacher other than the two football coaches. (Let me interrupt this pity party to say I should have tried harder to make friends, to fit in at Winder. Nobody was "against" me. My having played at Statham didn't matter to anyone. As an adult I realize that, but I was so eaten up with angst and resentful because of the senseless move from Statham that I couldn't see it then.)

At least I was free after three o'clock in the afternoon when football season ended, and occasionally I would hitchhike to Statham and visit with my pals, but darkness came early so there wasn't much time. One day a man picked me up, asked me where I was going, and then said, "I need to go by Monroe, but I won't be there but a second." He drove to a sawmill and talked for more than an hour while I waited in his truck. It was dark when we reached Statham, and all I could do was cross the highway and hitchhike back to Winder. Harriette Robertson and I had one date after I moved to Winder, thanks to the generosity of a mutual friend with a car. We went to a drive-in theater in Athens. I wasn't sixteen, so I couldn't drive our family car.

We had lived in Winder about six months when Mother gave me the old familiar message. We were moving again. Our destination was Wellington, Alabama. This time I was pleased. I didn't like Winder, and whatever Wellington was it couldn't be any worse.

Wellington wasn't a town and it wasn't a village, and you had to stretch your imagination to call it a community. It was simply out in the country. But it was an important railroad junction. The Seaboard and the L & N crossed at Wellington, and military personnel from nearby Fort McClellan boarded passenger trains there. It was near Anniston and Gadsden, so civilization was at hand. We borrowed a small house trailer that belonged to my sister and her husband and lived in that oven until we could rent a house. The good news was that the house was brand new; the bad news was that it was a four-room mini without plumbing. We had an outdoor privy and caught rainwater in a cistern. We had only a small pan for bathing. I kept a bar of soap in a tree at a nearby creek and usually bathed there while skinny-dipping. (The soap was Ivory, so that when I dropped it, it wouldn't sink.) Despite its privations, I liked Wellington better than Winder.

I attended Alexandria High School, riding a school bus eight miles each way. I was still in the tenth grade. I met a lot of friendly kids such as James Phillips, Gary Phillips, Donald Arial, Red Brown, Sue Tune, Lynn Curvin, Fritz Smith, Dan Perry, Raymond Carden, Echols Bryant, Ted Boozer, and Sharon Garrard. It reminded me of Statham High. I was playing basketball during a free period when a man introduced himself to me. He was Lou Scales, the football coach. He asked me where I was from, learned that I had played football at Winder, and said he hoped I would play at Alexandria. Spring practice was about to begin.

"Coach, I can't help your football team," I told him. "I'm not a good player." I stopped short of saying no. Could the football experience at Alexandria be different from the football experience at Winder?

"I could tell from watching you play basketball that you've got athletic ability," he said. "Give football a try at Alexandria. You might be surprised at how well you can play."

I did and I was. During that spring practice period Coach Scales taught me the fundamentals, taught me to play football. He didn't just say tackle that guy or block that guy, he showed me how to block and tackle. He utilized my speed by putting me at right halfback in the split-T formation and at safety on defense. Heavenly days, I acquired the nickname "Speedy." That's what some of my teammates called me. Football at Alexandria High was fun and rewarding, not the confidence-draining exercise it had been at Winder High. My life throbbed with possibility, as it had at Statham.

Just a year after the boot camp debacle at Winder I was in the running for a starting position at Alexandria. Ervin Love, a senior, beat me out during preseason practice in 1952, my junior season, but I was a solid second-teamer, and I saw a lot of action and played in every game. We went undefeated during the regular season but lost to Anniston High by one point in the Turkey Bowl on Thanksgiving Day. (Alabama didn't have high school post-season playoffs at the time.)

I was a starter on a 6–3 team as a senior. I even ran back kickoffs and punts. I scored two touchdowns against Walnut Grove in the opening game of 1953 and remembered when I couldn't get out of my own way at Winder just two years before.

I was appreciative to football at Alexandria for helping me get my groove back, and I gave it all I had, but the season and grueling weeks of spring practice extracted all the sweat and aches and pains I was willing to give, so I didn't play basketball or baseball at Alexandria High, and the school didn't have a track team. Austin Peay, a little college in Tennessee, invited me to try out for its football team, but I realized my limits and said no thanks. In later years Coach Scales told me I could have played college football. It was the only time I ever thought he was wrong.

Lou Scales had played fullback for the great coach Frank Thomas on Alabama's 1945 team that beat Southern California in the Rose Bowl. He had turned down an offer to play for the Chicago Bears. He was solidly grounded in the sport and was a superb teacher of football. Coaching, after all, is teaching. He didn't scream, didn't curse. He instructed. He coached at Alexandria thirty-eight years (1948–85), and became a legend in Alabama high school football. His final team won the state championship, and he was voted the state's coach of the year.

I played in the first game ever held in what would eventually be named Lou Scales Stadium. I helped organize a fifty-year reunion of that 1952 team in 2002, and Coach Scales attended. He said something that meant the world to me: "You were a good football player, Clyde." There was a time I never thought I'd hear those words.

Less than a year later he was dead. He was eighty-four years old. My wife and I drove to Hamilton, Alabama, for his funeral. It was a one-day round trip of some 250 miles. Few of his old players made the pilgrimage, but I was one who did. He had more influence on my life than any male except my daddy.

In 2007 I was inducted into the Calhoun County Sports Hall of Fame (for my writing, certainly not for any athletic achievements). It was especially gratifying because I joined my old coach, Lou Scales, who had been a charter inductee two years before. Who could have dreamed such a thing when he was inviting a shaky tenth grader to play on his football team?

IT WAS AT Alexandria High that I met my future wife, Sandra. She was a vivacious little thing whose high school resume includes being a majorette, Miss Homecoming, and captain of the Pep Squad. She was beautiful and immensely popular. I fell deeply in love, and so did she.

I proposed to Sandra in the kitchen of her friend Sue Tune's house. She was washing dishes and I was drying. It wasn't under moonlight and magnolias, but it stuck. We have three sons, Mike, Mark, and Mitch, and four grandchildren, Cory, Lauren, Lily, and Hannah Bolton. We've had a wonderful, nourishing marriage. We were in love when we married more than fifty-five years ago, and we're still in love. She's the best thing that ever happened to me, and she'll tell you I'm the best thing that ever happened to her.

But before marriage I began my ill-fated march toward what I believed would be a career in pharmacy, of all things. I enrolled at Jacksonville State University, and since my parents couldn't afford for me to stay on campus I drove sixteen miles a day in the aforementioned Kaiser, the one that was on life support in the form of used motor oil.

The Kaiser gave up, and shortly afterward I gave up, too. I quickly tired of bumming rides to and from Jacksonville. I had passed algebra at Alexandria High School, but I was dumbfounded by college algebra, and the teacher said I would have to sign up for what amounted to another high school course. I had no intention of taking a step backward, especially in a subject that doesn't exist in the real world. I began spending more time in the poolroom than the classroom. My lack of preparation, transportation, and motivation made academia seem a bad joke. I wanted to be married to my high school sweetheart and working at a job in that same real world. I didn't even complete my freshman year before I dropped out of college.

A few days later I got the break that opened the door to a writing career. At the time it didn't seem like much of a break, though. I was looking for a job, any job, in Anniston and Gadsden, walking the streets, knocking on doors. Sears didn't need anyone and neither did Goodyear, the phone company, the power company, Belk's, the post office, a hardware store, or any of a dozen other places of business. The *Anniston Star* did need someone. It needed a flunky in the circulation department, and it would pay $39.50 a week. I took the job, and on May 5, 1955, a forty-six-year career in the newspaper business began unceremoniously.

It was dirty, menial work. I did whatever needed to be done, from sweeping the sidewalks to keeping records to delivering papers to homes the carrier boys missed to running errands to taking the papers off the press. The last, performed in an un-air conditioned building out back, was particularly unpleasant. Each carrier handed me a slip of paper indicating how many newspapers he wanted. The papers came off the press into my arms, I fanned them out and counted them by twos with my thumb and handed them to each carrier. It was impossible to keep up with the press, but I tried. I didn't wear a shirt because it would have been covered with ink. I joked that I could have held a mirror up to my chest and read the front page of the *Anniston Star*. I began haunting the newsroom, the sports department in particular, in my spare time. I was fascinated by the news-gathering operation. Now there, I thought, was something I would enjoy doing. John Cathey, the sports editor, said the paper needed coverage of church league softball. The *Star* wouldn't pay me, but the league would give me three bucks a night to be the official scorer. So I became a published writer by typing four-paragraph stories about softball games.

I was looking through the classifieds in the *Atlanta Constitution* one day when a help-wanted ad seemed to shout at me. The *LaGrange Daily News* in Georgia needed a sports editor. I applied for the job, and for a reason known only to God, was hired. In October of 1955 I became the sports editor of a daily newspaper. I had just turned nineteen. I made forty-five dollars a week and had a wife to support, but I covered the state champion LaGrange High School football team. I was just two seasons removed from my own playing days. We moved into a three-room furnished apartment, and for the first time I wasn't living in my parents' home. It was an adventure. The first thing Sandra did was buy a bucket of paint and a paint brush. It was always the first thing she did, wherever we lived. It's amazing what a coat of paint will do for a dump.

I found that I could write. I look back on some of those first stories at LaGrange and they're not bad. There were signs of amateurism, of course, clichés, over-dramatization, but as I gained experience at the *Daily News* my writing smoothed out. I used a writer's best tool—the simple declarative sentence—and my stuff required a minimum of polishing from Phil Harrison, the editor.

Eventually, I asked to be transferred from sports to main news in LaGrange. A small paper is a great place to learn the newspaper business because you handle so many different chores—writing stories, writing headlines, laying out pages, editing copy, shooting photos—and I wanted to be exposed to everything. I covered city hall, the courthouse, the cops, anything that moved. I welcomed civic club luncheons because I got a free meal.

Sandra and I stayed in LaGrange seventeen months. I went to the *Gadsden Times* and became city editor and to the *Montgomery Advertiser* and became state editor. But I didn't want to be an editor. I wanted to be a writer. Plus, working six nights a week at the *Advertiser*, trying with the aid of one assistant and a few amateur correspondents to keep up with everything in south Alabama, was as hopeless as trying to hem up balls of mercury on a table.

One day I drove to Birmingham and asked John Bloomer, the managing editor of the *Birmingham News*, for a job. Nothing was available in main news, he said, but the sports department needed a man. I had been out of sports five years, but I was sick of working at the *Montgomery Advertiser*, and I took it. On September 4, 1961, at age twenty-five, I reported for work at the state's biggest newspaper. I would stay forty years and three days before I retired on September 7, 2001.

Chapter 16

My home phone rang a year or so ago, and it was Bill Curry, the former Georgia Tech and Alabama football coach. "Guess where I am," he said. "I'm driving through Statham."

I play in an annual golf tournament for friends of University of Georgia football, and Vince Dooley, the former coach and director of athletics, never fails to say, "I suppose you stopped in Statham on the way, didn't you?"

My love for Statham is well known, and I'm pleased that it is. If I love a town or a friend or a barbecue joint or a dog or an old pair of shoes I say so. It doesn't embarrass me.

During my forty years at the *Birmingham News* I made it known that I would like to cover Auburn's and Alabama's football games against Georgia in Athens so I could visit Statham. I'd lobby for other events in Athens, too. I remember covering a Southeastern Conference track meet at the university and standing at the finish line and quivering as Herschel Walker ran the hundred meters. I wondered how any defensive back could bring himself to get in front of that human dragster. I remember covering an NCAA basketball regional in Georgia's coliseum and silently pulling against Marquette because one of its players walked out during the singing of the National Anthem.

The first football game I ever covered for the *Birmingham News* was Georgia-Alabama in Athens on September 23, 1961. It was the opener for both teams. Alabama's Bear Bryant was headed for a national championship, but Georgia's new coach, Johnny Griffith, who succeeded Wally

Butts, wasn't even at the game. Griffith suffered an attack of appendicitis and had surgery on Friday. Someone wrote that Griffith made his debut as Georgia's coach flat on his back, and his team soon joined him in that position. Alabama won 32–6.

I didn't visit Statham on that trip, though, because I was accompanying Benny Marshall, the sports editor of the *Birmingham News.* Benny wrote the game story, and my assignment was to write the post-game locker room stuff. Benny had hired me nineteen days before, and he was the best boss I had ever had or ever would have, and I wasn't about to suggest he chauffeur me on a nostalgia drive through the streets of Statham. I did mention one of my boyhood feats as we waited for the kickoff: "When I was a kid I used to hitchhike to Athens and climb over the fence at that end of the stadium." Benny smiled and said, "Why don't you try it now? I'll write a story about you when you break your neck or they put you in jail." No thanks.

WHEN I JOINED Benny's staff at the *Birmingham News* I expected to be assigned to high school sports, maybe some small college stuff. I was so pleased to be escaping the *Montgomery Advertiser* that I made no demands or even suggestions. I had been out of sports for five years, covering main news, and I didn't figure I had a case to plead.

Benny shocked me by immediately assigning me to major college coverage. During football season that meant that I wrote Alabama and Auburn features and advances during the week and covered the Tide or Tigers or some other Southeastern Conference team on Saturdays. I was delighted when Benny sent me to New Orleans to cover that 1961 Alabama team in the Sugar Bowl and to Miami to cover the 1963 Auburn club in the Orange Bowl. It was high cotton for a young man who had moved a lot but hadn't ever been anywhere. We weren't in Edgemoor, South Carolina, or Wellington, Alabama, Toto. The job would subsequently dispatch me to New York, Los Angeles, Kansas City, Boston, Chicago, Salt Lake City,

Philadelphia, Phoenix, St. Louis, Houston, and Dallas, among other major cities. I would cover the Super Bowl, the World Series, the Masters, the Indianapolis 500, the Daytona 500, and the NCAA basketball Final Four. I reckon I covered five hundred football games in my four decades at the *News*, including some memorable national championship bowls.

Benny was passionate about writing and so was I, and a bond developed between us. Benny wasn't old enough to be a father figure to me, but he was like a big brother, and we appreciated our respective roles in our relationship. Some newspaper writers are just picking up a paycheck, figuring their stories will be on the floor of a birdcage covered with parakeet poop the next day anyway. Others are like Benny and me. We'd spend fifteen minutes staring at the typewriter, trying to summon the precise word. If an article had his name on it Benny wanted it to be as good as possible, and I shared his philosophy.

But Benny was a troubled man, an empathetic person who truly worried about the damaged world we live in, about people in Birmingham and in Vietnam. He covered the Auburn-Wake Forest football opener in 1969, but he never covered another game. The next Thursday he pressed a .38 revolver to his temple and pulled the trigger. He was gone and I was devastated. The eight years we spent together were among the most satisfying of my life.

Shug Jordan was the Auburn football coach when I arrived at the *News*. He had been one of Wally Butts's assistants at Georgia, and he was amused when I told him about scaling the fence at Sanford Stadium. Jordan and Bryant were different types in their relationship with the folks who covered their games. Jordan got along well with the press, even seemed to like most of us. Bryant was distant, frequently uncooperative, before he mellowed in his old age. I believe Bryant was the greatest college football coach who ever lived but of the two, Jordan was much more companionable. I covered Bryant for twenty-two seasons and Jordan for fifteen.

In my early years the *Birmingham News* didn't have a beat system, as it and most other papers do today. I covered both Auburn and Alabama during the week and on Saturdays and consequently knew coaches and athletes at both schools and made lasting friendships. When I was in Auburn I'd always drop by the office of a young assistant coach named Vince Dooley. He was intelligent and an interesting conversationalist in a variety of subjects. I was delighted when he became Georgia's head coach in 1964. Dooley resurrected the faltering program and was later a progressive, innovative director of athletics.

BENNY MARSHALL REALIZED that interest in stock car racing was increasing dramatically, and in 1962 he told me I was to be the paper's first racing writer. I tried to beg off, pleading that I knew nothing about racing. "You'll learn," Benny said, and I did. In Statham we had played football in Wayne Holliday's backyard, basketball on the "court," and baseball on the skinned diamond behind the school, and never gave car racing a thought except for speeding our bikes around an imaginary track on Broad Street for a couple of days after we'd heard the radio broadcast of the Indy 500. If anyone had told me racing would become my favorite sport I would have said he was nuts, but it happened.

I was the paper's racing writer from 1962 to 1990 and it was fun. The drivers were colorful characters, almost to a man bootstrap Southerners, and they were accessible to the press, grateful for the publicity. They drove souped-up automobiles that began life as real passenger cars. You could tell a Ford from a Chevrolet from a Plymouth.

And I was in the middle of it. Birmingham had the world's biggest, fastest track, Talladega Superspeedway, in its front yard, and some of the greatest drivers in its backyard. Hueytown, a Birmingham suburb, became known as the biggest little city in racing. It was home to Bobby Allison, Donnie Allison, Davey Allison, and Neil Bonnett, who among them won 131 races in what is now Sprint Cup, and who were known collectively as the Alabama Gang.

I have little interest in the NASCAR of today. It's a greedy, money-driven, made-for-TV undertaking. The drivers aren't as colorful or as friendly, and the cars are cookie-cutter creations, crafted so that no make has an edge. One of the lures of old-timey racing was that a fan could pull for his favorite brand (win on Sunday, sell on Monday, the manufacturers used to say), but that makes no sense now because they are one hundred per cent racing machines, not Fords or Chevrolets or Dodges or Toyotas.

And there's no Alabama driver on the circuit. I was reading a race lineup in the paper and I remarked to Sandra, "During the heyday of the Alabama Gang, would you have believed the time would come when there'd be no Alabamians, but three drivers from Las Vegas in a race?" It's like watching Little League when your son is playing and then trying to maintain interest after he has moved on.

Racing did furnish the most remarkable sports figure I ever met, William Henry Getty "Big Bill" France, the founder of NASCAR, the builder of Daytona International Speedway and Talladega Superspeedway. France was a high school dropout, a service station mechanic and part-time racecar driver who became the most influential person in American motorsports. His life turned tragic in his later years, though. We had become fast friends, and I was excited when he asked me to write his biography, but Alzheimer's disease intervened, and it never happened. He died and a treasury of great stories died with him.

France's illness and death and what I called the Hueytown Horrors also contributed to my waning interest in racing. Donnie Allison's career was effectively ended by a crash in 1981. A devastating wreck in 1988 left Bobby Allison fighting for his life, and he never raced again. In 1992 his son, Clifford, was killed in a racing practice wreck. In 1993 his other son, Davey, died in a helicopter crash. Neil Bonnett lost his life in a practice accident in 1994. Grant Adcox and Dale Earnhardt were other friends who became victims of racing. Even though I stopped being the racing beat man in 1990, I continued to write columns about the sport, and toward the end I dreaded going to the track.

Racing provided the most memorable sports event I ever covered, though. Bobby Allison won the 1988 Daytona 500 with his son, Davey, on his bumper. I rushed to find wife and mother Judy Allison and interviewed her.

A lot happened to change the fabric of sports in Alabama during my forty years at the *News*. The number one sociological change, of course, was racial integration. Sports for women also became a reality, thanks to Title IX. The most impressive physical change was construction of the racetrack at Talladega, which brought the state its only major league professional sport. Spacious new arenas at Alabama and Auburn and in Birmingham raised basketball to another level. UAB began playing football and basketball and fielding teams in other sports. Pro football teams came to Birmingham, but they didn't stay.

I covered so many greats that a sampling will have to do: Pat Sullivan, Terry Beasley, and Bo Jackson. Joe Namath, Snake Stabler, and John Hannah. Archie, Peyton, and Eli Manning. Bill Stanfill, Terry Hoage, and Champ Bailey. Pete Maravich, Dominique Wilkins, and Michael Jordan—when he played baseball with the Birmingham Barons. Adolph Rupp, Steve Spurrier, and Pat Summitt. Richard Petty, David Pearson, and Darrell Waltrip. Arnold Palmer, Gary Player, and Lee Trevino. Dale Murphy, Reggie Jackson, and George Brett.

I became a sports columnist for the *Birmingham News* in 1970 and wrote columns until I retired in 2001. Readership surveys showed they were immensely popular, and that led to a distinction that I'm not so much proud of as amused by: There may have been more readings of my writing than of any other Alabamian's in history. When I was studying English under Miss Sue Perkins in Statham I couldn't have dreamed that would be the case.

Eighteen books—six fiction and twelve nonfiction—have contributed to the total. One day the head of a publishing company walked into my office unannounced, said he liked my newspaper work and asked if I'd write a book for him. The result was *The Crimson Tide*, a history of University of Alabama football. In the thirty-seven years since, I've usually been planning, writing, or promoting a book.

Sports writing changed over the years, and it wasn't as much fun as it had been. When my career began the focus was on the games. There was little critical, in-depth reporting. The athletes were heroes—frequently described as "gallant" if they put up a good fight in defeat. The sportswriters collectively made up what the rest of the news staff called the Toy Department. But eventually the sports scene came to be covered like anything else: the police beat, city hall, the legislature. The slant today is on the gratuitously negative, finding a cloud on every silver lining, and I wonder if little boys in Statham still view sports through gee-whiz rose-colored glasses, as we did.

The influence of the Internet and talk shows and cable TV and Watergate contributed to newspapers covering sports in the uninspiring modern way. Watergate? Sure. A herd of boys and girls in journalism school realized if they could bring down a president they could certainly level a quarterback, and without even donning a helmet. Of course, the modern sports scene does require edgier coverage. Athletes are constantly in trouble with the law. The dopehead ballplayer is a cliché. Take a sorry individual and pay him ten million dollars and you get a punk who can afford to become enormously sorry. And it's difficult to portray overpaid athletes who go on strike for still more money as residing on Olympus. Owners who threaten to move their teams if they don't get a new stadium or arena when there's nothing wrong with the old one are extortionists.

I WAS READY to retire when I turned sixty-five in 2001. I'd still write books, and that would be enough. I wouldn't have to sort through the controversy and unrest that continually infected Alabama's and Auburn's sports programs—and I wouldn't have to battle the creeping convoy of traffic that gets worse with each expansion of a stadium or race track. I haven't been to a football game at Auburn or Tuscaloosa or a race at Talladega since I retired, and I won't be going in the future. The boy who woke up itching to hitchhike to Athens to see the Bulldogs play became the man who on Saturday prefers TV games and a can of beer and a steak grilling on the patio to gridiron gridlock.

A final reflection on Statham and its exile: I was dispirited, heartbroken, when we moved. But do I wish I had never left? No. As Archie Fant, my fictional policeman, told my cow kidnapers, the years teach much which the days never know.

I met and married a wonderful Alabama girl, and for more than half a century Sandra and I have laughed together when the going was good and supported each other when the going was bad, and we will until death does us part.

I became a newspaperman, and my job with the *Birmingham News* enabled me to see the United States, to cover marquee sporting events, to meet the greats of sport, to twice be invited to the White House by presidents of the United States, all on an expense account. Writing for the paper led me into writing books, and I would rather be a writer than anything else.

How could I wish none of that had happened?

Did I ever consider moving back to Statham? Not seriously. Oh, I used to wonder if I might return when I retired, but deep down I knew I wouldn't. Our three sons and four grandchildren all live within a few miles of us. So do most of our dearest friends. It would make no sense to leave, especially at this late stage of our lives.

And I remember something Mother said: "Your daddy lived in Statham when he was a boy, and he always wanted to move back, but when he moved back he wasn't happy. It wasn't the same." It wouldn't be the same for me, either. None of our little gang lives there. Harriette Robertson Young Nowell, Rose Marie Herrin Salzer, Wayne Holliday, Buck Manus, and Chick Bragg are dead. Gayle Mobley Ferguson lives in Winder, Emma Lou Owens Rowden near Watkinsville, and Jimmy Lowe in Madison, Mississippi. Mr. Barrett, Miss Perkins, and Aunt Eva wouldn't be there to counsel me. The high school is gone and so are Perry's Pond, the Royal Theater, and Fannie Mae's cafe.

Years ago, when I was working for a boss who could have been the poster boy for the Peter Principle, I seriously considered buying a house in Statham, to use as a getaway when I had free time. When I telephoned the owner she was drunk and made no sense. I didn't call back. I later learned she sold the house for several thousand dollars less than the offer I had in mind.

I'm glad she was drunk. Owning two homes 208 miles apart would have been a terrible financial, physical, and emotional strain that inevitably would have ended in disappointment. It was a Broad Street oldie, and I don't have the handyman knowledge or skill required to keep one of those beauties in the state of preservation it deserves. A friend of mine bought a place on Logan Martin Lake in Alabama so he could go fishing and boating in his spare time—but he spends all his spare time working on the house and the yard.

I enjoyed living in Statham, and I enjoyed reliving those days as I constructed this book. I relied largely on memory, mine and others', to recreate life in the late 1940s and early 1950's in a small Southern town. Memory isn't infallible, but I gave it an honest effort, and so did they.

I am reminded of something my friend, author, and movie connoisseur David Housel said about the classic westerns of director John Ford, films such as *Stagecoach*, *The Searchers*, and *The Man Who Shot Liberty Valance*:

"If that's not the way it was, it's the way it should have been."

About the Author

Clyde Bolton retired after forty years with the *Birmingham News*. Prior to that he had written and edited for the *Anniston Star*, *LaGrange Daily News*, *Gadsden Times*, and *Montgomery Advertiser*. He has also written eighteen books, been married for fifty-four years, and raised three sons. He and his wife, Sandra, live in Trussville, Alabama.